Hand, Reef and Steer

Tom Cunliffe

WATERLINE

Published by Waterline Books
an imprint of Airlife Publishing Ltd
101 Longden Rd, Shrewsbury, England

ISBN 1 85310 309 8

A Sheerstrake production.

A CIP catalogue record of this book
is available from the British Library.

Illustrations by John Glasspool.
Photographs by Tom Cunliffe unless otherwise indicated.

This book could not have been written without my wife, Ros.
To her it is lovingly dedicated, my mate and my fellow-rover.

ACKNOWLEDGEMENTS

It would never be possible to acknowledge all the sailors who have set me straight over half a lifetime, but one or two stand out. Some of these may be surprised to find themselves thus mentioned:

Martin Matthews, fellow schoolboy who first suggested that we might 'go for a sail.' W A Robinson, whose book *'Deep Water and Shoal'* sealed the arrangement. Steve Leach, my room-mate at university, who unwittingly taught me the real facts about sailing to windward. Captain Justin Avellar, whose ropes were extremely long and who could tell you kindly how to do any job — once. Ex-P.O. Bob Hall, whose seizings saw a very doubtful outfit safely over the ocean. Davey Elliot, foreman of the Elephant Boatyard, who is not tight-fisted with the jewels of his art. Captain Alec Smith who taught me more than anyone about the mechanics of modern yacht sailing. Ginny Jones and the boys at the old Mystic Mission to Seamen, who kept me out of the lunatic asylum, and Clark Poston, a great sailor who knows a lot more than I do about schooners.

Lastly, I am grateful to Patrick Selman of Southwest Sails, who understands how to cut a gaff mainsail.

❈❈❈❈❈❈❈❈

Those words marked with an asterisk * in the main text, may be found fully explained in an alphabetically arranged glossary in Appendix 2 on page 166.

CONTENTS

Kirsty, *a fine cruising ketch which has crossed the Atlantic with a husband and wife crew.*

INTRODUCTION

In the days before the Second World War, a number of excellent books were in print which guided their readers through the techniques for going to sea in gaff-rigged boats and yachts. In the 1920s, the Bermudan alternative to gaff was in its infancy, so that any written work on sailing and seamanship referred to the four-cornered mainsail as the normal state of affairs. The tall, comparatively flimsy 'Marconi' rig that would ultimately replace it, was seen by many as a craze which, despite its obvious benefits, would 'never catch on'.

For better or worse, however, Bermudan rig took hold like a forest fire, so that by the 1950s anyone ordering a new yacht with a gaff rig would have been considered eccentric. After a further quarter of a century, the eclipse had become total. With the exception of a commercially insignificant group of enthusiasts, gaff-rig sailors were an extinct breed.

At that time there existed a very real danger that the traditional sailing skills kept alive by a few would die with their retirement from the water. The books from the earlier years would still be available in antiquarian bookshops, but reading a manual produced for a generation long gone, in circumstances that differ greatly from those of today, can never be a proper substitute for 'hands on' learning.

When I began sailing in the 1960s there were any number of yachtsmen who had first doused a topsail in a squall in the days when gaff rig was all that was available. Their knowledge was instinctive, and that made a tremendous difference. Such people are now comparatively rare, so that the sailor who chooses to put out to sea in a heavy-displacement vessel with sails and spars whose concept predates his own experience by a whole era, has either to learn by his mistakes, or rely on yesterday's written material.

It is to make good this lack of contemporary information that I have decided to write this book. The core material of the contents is a couple of centuries old, but I hope the presentation will suit the rapidly growing numbers of us who will be sailing our timeless craft into the third millenium.

With the exception of a few recently developed yachts whose designers believe they can offer the best of both worlds, the average gaffer, ancient or modern, is a long-keeled vessel with a deep forefoot. The way this sort of hull suits the rig, and vice versa, will be considered later in the book, and many references will be made to the manner in which the behaviour of such a boat differs radically from the cut-away fin-keeled yachts of the late twentieth century.

Understanding the hull is half the secret of handling a traditional craft. The earlier works on the subject make little, if any reference to this, because in the 1920s or 30s, all sailing boats had long keels, and even the most avant-garde ocean racer displaced up to twice as much as many production cruisers of our own period. Anyone weaned on 'fin and spade' performance yachts who goes to sea in a hull whose form is not significantly different from that of a nineteenth century working vessel is in for some surprises. Most of these will be pleasant. However, forewarned is forearmed, so I make no apologies for this aspect of the contents.

The book has no pretensions to being a sailing primer. It assumes a basic knowledge of the rudiments of how a boat converts airflow into drive through the water. For that reason, the reader should be able to 'dip in' at any section which seems likely to be useful.

I apologise at the outset to lady readers, for using the masculine forms of the third person singular pronouns referring to sailors, skippers, and crew members. This implies no presumption that traditional sailing is a male preserve. Any sane observer would know that this has not been so for decades. However, to write 'he or she' throughout a book is clumsy, and makes the English hard to read. In this respect, I fear that our language is proving inadequate for the times, and any masculine pronouns should be read as referring to either the male, or the female of our species.

I have tried to maintain a logical progress in the format of the chapters, but with so comprehensive a subject, where a statement concerning one aspect begs a nodding acquaintance with another, this ideal has not always been attainable.

After a discussion about the history of gaff, and some thoughts on how it fits in to the current sailing scene, the book moves on to describe the rig's components and how they should work together in harmony. Thereafter we get down to the exciting part of actually making the sailing of these wonderful craft both enjoyable and effective. I have endeavoured to draw as much as possible from my own experience of different types of boat, but since I have spent considerable time in the last ten years working a Bristol Channel Pilot Cutter, you will notice many references to these fine vessels. Fortunately, they are typical of main-stream gaff rig in its closing days, so I see no harm in giving them more than a passing mention.

Anyone can achieve reasonable passages in a production Bermudan sloop. It takes a sailor to extract the best from a gaffer, so stand by to slip the mooring; let's get under way.

The gaff yawl Duet *in Cowes Roads.*

CHAPTER I

GAFF IN PERSPECTIVE

Since we are going to spend the next sixteen chapters talking about how gaff rig works, it seems a good idea to spare a thought at the outset for the origins of the whole affair. There are so many theories about where the gaff itself came from that some of them, at least, must be right. The truth is that it developed from different beginnings in diverse parts of the world. The best features of the various forms were incorporated into the state-of-the-art rigs that were eclipsed by the arrival of the internal combustion engine and the Bermudan revolution.

One interesting proposition is that the gaff grew out of the sprit rig, seen today in numerous small traditional craft, as well as the Thames Sailing Barge.

The advantage of the large spritsail is its ability to be handled by a light crew. This stems from the fact that no one has the job of hoisting it. It stays up permanently, and is stowed by a system of brails*. If numbers are no problem, this becomes less important, and you will be more bothered by the way the sail's shape is compromised at any time it is setting to windward of the sprit. In an evolutionary attempt to circumvent this nuisance, the heel of the sprit began to move up the mast in certain craft, notably in Holland, until it reached the same position as the throat of a 'modern' gaff. As the heel rose higher, the angle of the sprit became flatter, which made it resemble a gaff still further.

Once the spar had reached the vicinity of the hounds, it only needed gaff jaws, a lacing for the head of the sail, and throat* and peak* 'lifts', to become a 'standing' gaff.

This arrangement has been employed within living memory by substantial vessels, including *Tern IV*, the famous 60ft cutter designed by Claude Worth. Her crew were enjoying not having to hoist their main right up to the 1970s.

After the gaff had arrived, it was only a short jump to rig it with running throat and peak halyards. The job was rounded off by slinging a boom under the foot of the sail to maintain its shape off the wind.

Another obvious origin of gaff rig lies with the lug sail.

Until recently, luggers have been written off by yachtsmen as hopelessly inefficient craft, unworthy of consideration. They could not have been more wrong. Lugsails started their career in the mists of pre-history, but by the 1880s and 90s they had attained a zenith of pure, straight-line performance that was never surpassed by a working vessel. Well into the twentieth century, the multi-tiered three-masted Bisquines of Brittany could show their sterns to just about anything afloat.

In their prime, the big luggers could lay within 4 points* of the wind, which is as close as a modern cruising yacht, and some of their passage times indicate average speeds in excess of nine knots.

Unfortunately, lug rig was desperately labour intensive, with heavy flax mainsails of near tennis-court proportions needing to be hoisted by hand, or latterly, by steam capstan. Such a sail could be highly dangerous if an inexperienced man took a turn off a cleat at the wrong moment.

Like the spritsail, a lug only set to perfection with the yard to leeward of the mast, so it had to be dropped, manoeuvred round the mast and rehoisted at every tack or gybe. Even if sea room were plentiful, this was a serious misery on a dark, rainy night in a rising gale. For the 80-footers working to windward up the narrow guts off the East Anglian coast it was so burdensome that by the 1870s, many were scrapping their fore-lugs and replacing them with a primitive gaff arrangement known as 'dandy' rig.

A dandy-rigged smack substituted her lug-yard with a very long gaff. The sail was set loose-footed, but it was laced or hooped to the mast. These early craft had no main boom, but unlike the lug, the gaff was hoisted and lowered with throat and peak halyards. A headsail was carried forward of the mast to balance things up, and the transformation was complete. From lugger to gaffer in a two-week refit. Booms arrived later as a useful refinement. Even though a dandy was a knot slower than a lugger, the compromise was welcomed by the hard-bitten realists of the fishing community.

The efficient, well-organised working yacht rigs which we recognise today followed rapidly on the heels of these, and all the other early forms. Like the clipper ship and the steam locomotive, they flowered as roses in summer. Their good fortune was that, unlike the big ships, whose budding perfection was superseded in their own time by overblown, box-sectioned sailing warehouses, the small craft were pruned neatly, at the height of their blooming, by the internal combustion engine and the yachtsman's search for windward performance.

That the change-over was executed in one generation for all but a few exceptional types, says everything. Let's look at one example. It would take considerable engine power to drive a 50ft Bristol Channel Pilot Cutter at the 9 knots she can reach with her sails under ideal circumstances. Far less is required to shove her through the water at a comfortable 6 nautical miles per hour, regardless of calms or moderate head-winds. The day when you can run 150 miles from noon to noon under sail alone is the exception rather than the rule. Install a 100HP motor, and you can guarantee it in all but the most contrary weather. The benefits this opened up to water-borne commerce are too enormous to quantify, but are best summed up by a line in a song about the steam drifter:

'No need to wait for wind or tide,
You're the master of the sea.'

Before the engine achieved its ascendancy in the early 1900s, no one could have made such a claim.

For the yachting fraternity, the situation was different, and still is. Yachtsmen and women go to sea for pleasure, fulfilment, personal discovery, or for any other reason you care to name, other than that it makes sense.

Man is placed aside from the beasts of the field by his ability to alter the environment. On land he has achieved awesome results, but it is to the earth that we are ultimately bound. We may plough the fields, build dwellings to shelter from wind and rain, and plant crops with which to fill our bellies, but we will never change the sea. At least so far as sail is concerned. Only there can we live in surroundings whose elemental nature has not been cut back and blunted to shore up our own inadequate survival capabilities. That is its enormous attraction for the amateur sailor.

If the moon has dictated that the tide will ebb for six hours, there is absolutely nothing we can do to stop it happening. An onshore gale, or a windless day are beyond our control, yet both affect our actions totally.

The working seaman accepted such things from birth. He developed his skills and his vessels to extract the maximum progress compatible with his continued security, but he never lost sight of what could, and could not be attempted. It isn't surprising that this insight has generally been denied to our generation. We are surrounded by unnatural wonders. We see gravity defied daily by the aircraft which fly overhead. Men walk on the moon, and auxiliary yachts can proceed directly into the eye of the wind for hour after hour.

Mankind's deep-rooted desire to outface the elements led not only to the development of the engine, it was also the source of most advances in yacht design. From their first beginnings, purpose-built yachts were potentially faster and more close-winded than working vessels, even though a few highly successful ones began their lives as fishing boats, pilot cutters, or general purpose knockabouts.

Bermudan rig arrived on the scene in the 1920s. By the outbreak of World War II its acceptance by racers and cruisers alike was almost complete, despite the inevitable reactionary resistance of much of the older generation and universal concern about the security of the new tall, thin spars. The fact that this revolution took only 15 years to come about, should serve to silence any argument about which type is generally superior for yachting purposes.

Since 1945, yachting has enjoyed steadily expanding horizons, yet virtually no gaff-rigged vessels have been built on speculation. Why then, do veteran and vintage yachts and workboats, classics and otherwise, find themselves and their gaff rigs becoming more and more popular? Why are an increasing number of custom builders turning their innovative talents to recreating the type of yachts that history has cast aside for apparently the best of reasons?

The deep, long keel of the traditional vessel is a crucial part of her handling characteristics.

I suspect that the motive may be pure nostalgia, but there is nothing to apologise for in that. One of the reasons that most of us go sailing is to put a bit of reality back into our lives. In our shore-side existence, we are cushioned almost completely from the world in which we were designed to live.

Until recently, even landsmen were governed by the turning seasons. The globe was of unimaginable immensity, and distance was walked out at 3 knots, or covered at 5 or 6 on horseback. A bad decision produced immediate repercussions which could give rise to physical discomfort, perhaps even death. Sailing brings us back to these values, but as yachts become ever more shiny, efficient and packed full of machines to insulate our bodies from having to work the foredeck, or our minds from the fear of navigational catastrophe, frustration has set in for many of us. The world we seek is the mysterious place in which men who could neither read nor write made their peace with wind and tide in order to feed their families. The lost asset which divides them from us was an understanding of their place in creation. The instantly recognisable symbol of that understanding is the gaff-rigged boat.

And that, for many of us, is what it's all about. We who go down to the sea in gaffers enjoy a double benefit. The boats fulfil the requirements of this peculiar inner demon, but fortunately that is not all they do. They also supply us with a highly seaworthy, reliable and beautiful means of everyday sailing transport; so if some of them aren't quite as fast to windward in calm water as a modern flyer, what matter to us?

It was inevitable that the obvious windward superiority of Bermudan sails should initially have almost ousted gaff from the seas. However, a common mistake made by the unenlightened is that, compared with its replacement, gaff really didn't have much going for it at all. In fact, gaff has numerous advantages denied to the leg-of-mutton* brigade, over and above the purely esoteric questions we have been looking at. It is these advantages that raise the well-maintained 75-year-old gaffer beyond the status of a motor-car of similar age, and enable replicas to be rigged far nearer to the originals in all practical aspects than would otherwise be the case.

None but the most dedicated enthusiast would use a 1929 Bentley to make a grand continental tour on today's roads. It would be far too expensive. The car would also be draughty, noisy, frightening to insure, and exhausting to drive for 400 miles at a stretch when compared with its present-day equivalent. It is a glorious machine, nonetheless, but it is now relegated to 'occasional use' status, even though it may be life itself to its owner.

Traditional sailing vessels do not find themselves in this position. The owners of classic yachts and workboats employ them as their everyday water transport, just as if they were production craft. Remarkable voyages are undertaken by elderly vessels, and those who make them are generally more than satisfied with the service given by their boats.

Heavy, long-keeled craft are far more comfortable at sea than their lighter sisters. They can be left to look after themselves in hard weather, so that as a crew becomes exhausted, the boat will take care of them. Many yachts of post-1980 design require

Hove to

The traditional gaff-rigged vessel settles down, pointing higher to wind and wave than her modern counterpart because - A) as her sail is reefed, the centre of effort remains well aft, unlike the Bermudan sail and B) the deeper forefoot of the traditional form grips the water and holds the boat's head up.

more attention from their people, rather than less, when survival conditions approach. A gaff-rigged boat with a deep forefoot* will heave-to in fair weather or foul, and point up high as she does so. The peace of mind that comes from knowing this manoeuvre is always available to defuse a nasty situation, or just to have a rest, is beyond the understanding of those who have not experienced it.

A boat with a serious displacement can carry more weight for her length than a lighter craft. This means that in addition to having no difficulty over stores and tank capacity, she can be properly equipped with ground tackle. Most cruising gaffers have comparatively low rigs with masts set well inboard; they also have an excellent grip on the water, even when being blown sideways from a standstill. The net result is that traditional vessels anchor beautifully, with far less likelihood of dragging than a boat with no draught to speak of, other than her keel and rudder.

Whether she is old or was built last year, the gear on a gaffer should be cheap to make and easy to replace. Gaff masts are generally reliable because they are heavily rigged and low down, but if you are unfortunate enough to lose a boom, a bowsprit, or a topmast, it is only a semi-skilled job to fashion a new one with a few simple tools. If the fittings have disappeared, the local blacksmith or welding shop can knock up replacements in a few hours. Try doing that with a buckled aluminium extrusion in a settlement north of the Arctic Circle!

The capacity for self-reliance doesn't end with the rig. Traditional craft, particularly working craft, were generally over-engineered because no one really knew how strong anything was, so they made their gear chunky in order to be sure. For this reason, failures can usually be fixed up by a determined team, even if specialised boat-building skills are not amongst their collective experience.

The use of tackles*, instead of winches is a tremendous plus for the old-fashioned sailor. Winches are expensive and noisy, they take up deck space, sometimes to the extent that it is impossible to carry a hard dinghy aboard a 45ft yacht, and sooner or later they fail. Wooden-cheeked blocks will work perfectly for half a century and more if they are cleaned and greased once a year, a task which takes about five minutes for a triple and two minutes for a single sheave block.

Because of its low aspect ratio, a gaff rig is less prone to stalling if oversheeted than something taller and narrower. This eases the tedium for the watch on deck.

The overriding advantage of gaff rig against Bermudan is that as soon as sheets are eased and the true wind moves beyond 60° from the bow, gaff is more powerful. Furthermore, because it is lower-slung, it does not strain a hull so severely for a given amount of drive. Gaff has the capability of spreading a large sail area from an easily-stayed mast. To achieve an equivalent amount of canvas from a three-cornered rig the mast must reach up to the heavens. For this reason, gaff is the logical rig for most heavy displacement craft which, by virtue of their mass, require a great deal of sail.

Notwithstanding this, many of today's heavy cruising yachts are saddled with a Bermudan rig which fails to suit their needs. A long, low aspect ratio keel does not encourage the high pointing that the Bermudan sail allows, so little is gained while much is lost. The perfect symbiosis of hull form and rig, on an original gaffer that has not been messed around, is a delight to all who sail in her, yet the lessons which such craft embody are consistently ignored by many of today's designers.

It must never be forgotten that while gaff rig and working-boat hulls were primitive when compared with a modern racing yacht, these old craft and their sail plans were at the end of a line of natural development which stretched back to the time of Christ. Neither builders nor owners were playing with the sea. They were in deadly earnest, and the yachtsmen of the day were heavily under the influence of their outlook. Any cynic who smiles patronizingly at an old gaffer would do well to consider the words of that great Irish circumnavigator, Conor O'Brien:

'These boats....were built by poor men for poor men, suffering from the two great spiritual evils of poverty — ignorance and prejudice. That they still produced fine boats is to the glory of natural man, who, living close to elemental things, develops an instinct for the earth or the sea which passes sophisticated understanding.'

A well-balanced gaffer is a dream to steer.

CHAPTER II

FORMS AND SPECIFICS

In this chapter we'll take a look at the basic gaff rig, the general way in which it is set up, and how the power to operate it is managed. I've chosen a cutter to illustrate the organisation of the gear, because it is the simplest form which embodies most of the essentials. Before becoming involved in specific details, however, we should perhaps consider where the cutter fits in with the rest of the gaff rig family.

THE CAT-BOAT

The simplest gaffer of all. The cat-boat sets a single gaff sail from a mast generally innocent of shrouds. It drives her beamy, shallow hull with remarkable efficiency. Cat-boats are usually in the 18–25ft bracket, though a hundred years ago certain working examples ran up to 40ft. Handling these must have been quite something, because in 1876 the sail on one recorded 27-footer boasted an area of 800 sq ft.

Cat-boats are a speciality of New England. The originals were general working craft, but the form was sufficiently successful to be adopted by the yachting community. They excel in shoal, sheltered waters, where their 3ft draught (board up) serves them well and the pure, powerful sail carries them closer to the wind than any other gaffer.

A boat which carries headsails will be unable to point quite so high as one with a main only. The headsails bend the air around the back of the main, which must always be set to leeward of amidships. If the headsails were arranged to sheet as close to the centreline of the boat as they are theoretically capable, they would hopelessly backwind the main. They are therefore sheeted further outboard, and pointing suffers in consequence. Cat-boats have none of this problem, so they just slice up to weather. Headsails give a boat added power, however, to say nothing of manoeuvrability. They also allow her sail area to be broken up into more manageable divisions. At sea, the cat-boat may suffer a lack of drive which is the pay-off for her pointing, while her heavy, mast tends to make her pitch.

As a post-script, in case you were thinking that with so huge a sail, such a vessel must be murder in the helm-balance department, the steering characteristics of a cat-boat can often be re-organised by adjusting the position of her centreboard for different points of sailing, as though she were a racing dinghy.

THE SLOOP

Historically, the term 'sloop' could mean any number of different types of craft. During the Napoleonic wars, for example, a British sloop of war was a small full-rigged ship*. The name defined her classification as a fighting vessel, and had nothing whatever to do with her rig. Since the last half of the nineteenth century, however, so far as yachts and commercial vessels have been concerned, a sloop has become a vessel having one mast, with a mainsail set from its after side and a foresail hanked to the forestay.

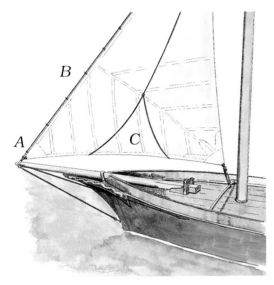

A typical sloop foretriangle

Note that the forestay is set up to the bowsprit, (A), the sail is hanked to the forestay, (B) and employs lazy jacks to facilitate stowage, (C).

A Friendship sloop in her home waters of Maine

A sloop is differentiated from a cutter not so much in the number of headsails she carries (although most smaller sloops employ only one), as in the nature and position of her bowsprit and forestay. In theory at least, a cutter has a retractable bowsprit. Her forestay is set up at, or even inboard of, the stemhead. If a sloop has a bowsprit, it is permanently rigged, and the main forestay is run to its outboard end.

Like the cat-boat, the sloop rig is rarely seen in Europe except in small yachts, although it has caught on like a forest fire in the world of Bermudan craft. In North America, however, the sloop has always been popular, with her large mainsail, her mast well forward, and an enormous jib complete with reef points tacked down to a comparatively short bowsprit.

Slocum's *Spray* was a sloop (despite her diminutive lug mizzen), and her descendants and relatives are still to be seen up and down the eastern seaboard of America.

THE CUTTER

The sloop is close-winded and fast in calm water, but in some cases, particularly when she only has a single headsail, she lacks power when the sea gets up. The cutter supplies all the drive you could ask for, with at least two big headsails working together to slot the air round the back of a fair-sized main and topsail.

The cutter generally steps her mast further into the boat than the sloop. This gives her a generous staysail. It also allows for a somewhat smaller mainsail than a comparable sloop. The bowsprit now becomes an additional spar, rather than something vital to the security of the rig. If a cutter carries away her bowsprit she may lose her topmast as a result, but the lower mast is just as secure as if the accident had not happened. The bowsprit serves but one purpose: to set sail. The jibs it supports perform wonders for powering up the staysail, which, in turn, supplies more zip to the air flowing through the slot behind the mainsail.

The 'double headsail' rig gives rise to tremendous flexibility, with the skipper's options for sail choice being multiplied when compared with those open to the commander of a sloop. The only price of all this efficiency is that the boat will be marginally less close-winded than a sloop or cat-boat. At sea, however, this is a small bill for all the power you need, delivered by reasonable-sized packages of sail. On the exposed lee shores of northern Europe, this made the cutter the most popular form for both the working gaffer and the yacht. Even where a two-masted rig was preferred, the double-headsail arrangement was still generally favoured.

THE KETCH

The only serious problem attached to the cutter as an operational proposition is that once her length rises above a certain figure, the size of her sails prohibits easy operation by a crew of a given strength. It therefore pays in certain circumstances to cut down the length of the mainmast, move it forward a trifle, then erect a mizzen well inboard and hang the balance of the sail area from that.

The trade-off is in terms of performance. A ketch does not develop nearly so much

19

The ultimate in power and sea-keeping ability. Provident, the Brixham Trawler.

windward efficiency as a cutter. Since gaff rig is not a notable close-hauled performer in today's terms, the gaff ketch is unlikely to be the best choice if this is important to you. Fortunately, there is a large body of right-minded men and women who could not care a fig for the last 5° of pointing, but who are anxious to avoid the danger of personal rupture which may be present with a cutter of similar tonnage, so the pretty ketch will live on in the face of this drawback.

The point at which a cutter ceases to be viable depends entirely upon who sails her, and in what conditions. Racing cutters in the halcyon days before the end of the nineteenth century ran up to 130ft overall. Their booms could be over 100ft long, and their sail area might be as much as 14,000sq ft. Such vessels shipped a crew of 50 professionals, and one can imagine that none of them were left idle for long. In this light, the idea of breaking up the rig of a 30-footer into two masts seems rather odd, but for a weak crew it could still make all the sense in the world.

A strong young couple sailing in the twenty-first century, even if they are not born to the sea, should have no difficulty with a 35ft cruising gaff cutter, given that the rig is properly organised and that the boat is well endowed with deck space. At the larger end of today's market, a cutter of about 50ft with a mainsail of 800sq ft ought to present no serious problems at any time to three competent adults, two of whom need not be unusually strong.

THE YAWL

If you're looking for an easy distinction between a yawl and a ketch it is this: conventionally at least, a ketch's mizzen is stepped forward of the rudder post, while that of a yawl stands abaft it.

The mizzen of a yawl is smaller than that of a ketch. The main purpose it serves in a gaffer is to shorten the boom of a cutter, and allow a mizzen staysail, albeit a small one, to be set when circumstances allow. The popularity of the yawl-rigged yacht probably arose as a result of the fact that for many years the rating rules allowed such mizzens to be 'free sail area'. Historically, one hidden blessing of the yawl was that it eased the pain of the alarmingly long booms of the larger cutters.

Some nineteenth-century dandy-rigged drifters were technically yawls, because they had left the old mizzen lug where it was after converting the mainmast to gaff. It was stepped a long way aft, and the sail was still sheeted to the old outrigger. This spar, incidentally, was the forerunner of the bumkin almost invariably seen on the 'modern' gaff yawl. A number of Breton fishing types adopted this rig, among them the Camaret langoustiers. These were sometimes known as 'Dundees'. The origin of this name can only be the English word 'dandy', since the Scots were among the last to convert their luggers. Even then, the port of Dundee was not notably progressive.

A yawl is usually a better sailer than a ketch and may well carry less weather helm than an equivalent cutter, particularly off the wind. Dropping the mizzen as the first sail reduction is more effective than putting in a cutter's initial reef, because it knocks out a large proportion of any weather helm that may be developing. On the other hand, while a ketch may be capable of sailing to windward after a fashion under her mizzen, balanced by a jib or staysail ('jib and jigger'), most yawls are less than willing to look up to the breeze once the main has been stowed.

THE SCHOONER

The true gaff schooner is a two-masted vessel, gaff-rigged on both masts, with the mainsail set on the after mast. Schooners with more than two masts always have their title pre-fixed with the number of masts they boast, as in '4-masted schooner'. A 'schooner' has just the two. If she carries squaresails on her foremast she becomes a topsail schooner, but if one of these were a course (sheeting to deck level and set from the lower yard), she would be a brigantine, and not a schooner at all. Gaff topsails are taken for granted and pass without comment in her title. Any sloppy talk of 'twin-masted schooners,', or 'gaff topsail schooners' is the final word in ignorance.

Schooners were used throughout the western world as working vessels of every type. They traded, they fished, and they carried pilots. They also made great pirate ships, and the early 'clipper' hull forms were developed from 'sharp' American schooners in the mid-nineteenth century. In many ways the finest flowering of the rig was in the USA and Canada, where the fishing schooners of the Grand Banks reached remarkable peaks with 140ft vessels such as the *Bluenose* and the *L A Dunton*.

The *Dunton* survives in Mystic Seaport Museum, and a superb replica of the original *Bluenose* still sails from Nova Scotia. To stand on their decks and contemplate the

The romance of the schooner. Defiance *sails past downtown Manhattan.*

sheer height of the topmast trucks is an unforgettable experience. How much more dramatic it would have been to see them racing home from the Banks in a cold northeaster, heeling steeply, lively as a pair of horses, logging 14 knots and cramming on still more sail to maximise both their profits and their honour.

Schooner yachts were popular on both sides of the Atlantic in the late nineteenth and early twentieth centuries, but in Europe they gradually gave way to the cutter. Not so in the States. There, schooners were racing successfully into the 1930s. Possibly, their popularity resulted from the suitability of the rig for the reaching conditions often experienced, but it seems just as likely to stem from the pure romance of the type.

Great designers such as John Alden and Murray Peterson produced schooners until quite recently, many of them surprisingly small and delicate, and most of them giving the lie to the old prejudice about schooners not going well to windward. No one who has seen the Olin Stephens-designed *Brilliant* work out to weather of a fleet of big classic yachts on a day when the spray is flying has any illusions on that score. In the English Channel, the smaller Peterson boat *Mary Bryant* has shown many a proud racing cutter the shortest route to the windward mark.

A schooner has a greater flexibility of sail combination than any other vessel of her size. Her performance can equal that of a cutter, yet she is sometimes as easy to handle as a ketch. With the exception of a number of delightful American bijoux, however, the rig does not usually suit craft of less than about 38ft.

The schooner rig is very strong for a number of reasons. It usually has a short bowsprit, its masts are comfortably into the boat so they can be stayed easily, and because they are tied together by the triatics*, they offer a measure of mutual support. In most cases, this overrides the advantage that if your masts are entirely independent, you are less likely to lose both in any one incident. When confronted with such a proposition, the typical schoonerman's response would be that it is preferable to lose neither. I recall asking the skipper of the Alden-designed *Lord Jim* whether he had sent his tall, slender topmasts down on deck when he was traversing the Southern Ocean. I expressed surprise when he gave a negative reply.

'I was right, though,' he responded, 'we took a heavy knock-down off the pitch of the Horn and everything on deck was swept away, including the spare spars. The topmasts were safe enough though. They only dipped into the water for a second or two....'

Having taken a brief look at the most important variations of gaff rig, it should be clear by now why much of this book will concentrate on the cutter. The cat-boat and the sloop are rarely seen today, and in any case, they are simpler than the cutter, so they are covered automatically. All the other types usually incorporate the so-called 'cutter foretriangle'. The ketch and yawl are complicated merely by a smaller additional rig, and while extracting the best from a schooner is an art-form perfected by few, the principles of operating most of her sails are the same.

Illustrated (overleaf) is a simplified representation of a Norwegian pilot cutter of the type created by Colin Archer*. She is about 40ft on deck and displaces around 17 tons. At that size, she requires a full complement of purchases* to operate her rig. Properly equipped, she could be comfortably sailed by 2 men without the need for any winches, except a windlass to cope with the ground tackle. For reasons of clarity, some of the purchases described below have been omitted from this particular illustration. If you want to get to the bottom of the business straight away, use the cross-referencing key to find the details illustrated elsewhere in the book. If you feel like an easier read, enjoy the description, then press on.

I have selected the Norwegian boat for this initial statement because she has such a simple pole mast. You'll notice that it carries only two shrouds per side and one forestay, but that it is massively proportioned, achieving most of its strength from sheer physical size. Like all traditional masts it is solid and stepped on the keel.

On a cutter, the jib(a) is traditionally set flying. The tack is attached to a hook on the traveller*, which is pulled to the bowsprit end using the outhaul. An inhaul is not generally necessary, because if the outhaul is let go on most points of sailing, the traveller is only too pleased to come inboard on its own.

The jib sheets are led down to the foredeck. There can be any number of arrangements for trimming them and these will be discussed in Chapter V.

The jib halyard is a classic arrangement. It is double-ended, passing through a single block shackled or hooked to the head of the sail with both falls* coming down to

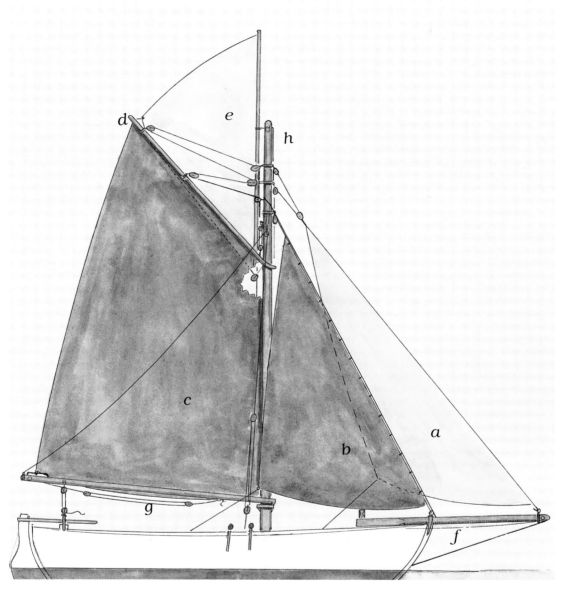

Representation of a Norwegian pilot cutter

Jib (a) Illustrated on page 25
Staysail (b)
Mainsail (c) Illustrated on page 56
Gaff (d) Illustrated on page 33

Topsail (e) Illustrated on page 65
Bowsprit (f) Illustrated on page 31
Boom (g) Illustrated on page 37
Masthead (h) Illustrated on page 29 & 33

the deck. One fall is the hauling part. When you are heaving on this end, the other part is left made fast, with the result that you achieve a 2:1 purchase (see Chapter V). When you've got all you can with that end, it is made fast so that you can transfer your attentions to the other fall. This is spliced onto a tackle, or purchase, rigged between the fall of the halyard and the deck. By pulling on this you benefit not only from whatever the power of the purchase may happen to be, but also from the 2:1 of the fall of the halyard. 4:1 is often chosen. The two powers are multiplied, which leaves you with 8:1 in all.

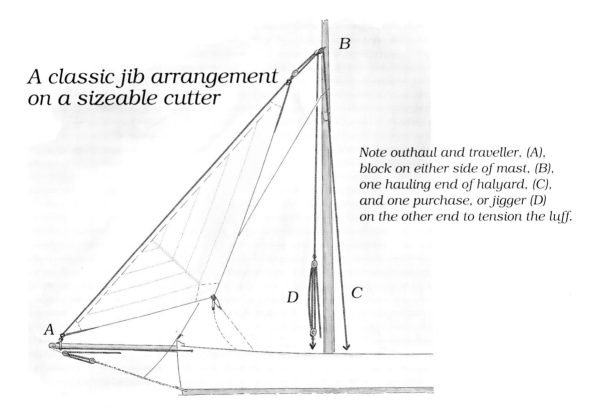

A classic jib arrangement on a sizeable cutter

Note outhaul and traveller, (A), block on either side of mast, (B), one hauling end of halyard, (C), and one purchase, or jigger (D) on the other end to tension the luff.

Moving aft from the jib, the staysail(b) is shackled to the stemhead and hanked to the stay. Its halyard is rigged like that of the jib, except that in this case it has one double block up the mast instead of two singles. Some staysails are set on a small boom, which allows them to be self-tending when tacking. This one is loose-footed. There are benefits to both arrangements which we'll look into in Chapter VIII. If the sail is loose-footed, its sheeting arrangements are generally similar to those for the jib.

The mainsail (c) on this craft is set loose-footed on its boom. The tack is secured at the goose-neck*, while the clew is loosely shackled to a horse* on the top of the boom, and tensioned by the outhaul. This passes round a turning sheave* at the extreme outboard end and is adjusted by means of a tackle rove off under the boom. The same tackle is often used to heave down the reef pendants*. Some loose-footed mains have their tacks set up by a downhaul, and this will be described in Chapter VI.

The gaff(d) is hoisted by throat and peak halyards which are often double ended on a vessel of this tonnage with purchases rigged on the standing ends as was the case with the headsail halyards. The purchases may not be used when hoisting the sail in ideal conditions but, as we shall see, they are priceless when jigging up the gaff after shaking out a reef at sea, particularly if the sail is full of wind.

On Colin Archer boats the mainsheet invariably utilises a thwartships horse. The system has the advantage that when the boat is close-hauled the upper block is directly above the lower one. This means that if the sheet is hove down really hard, the pull goes right up the leech of the sail and helps to hold the gaff up to windward. This has proved one of the best ways of preventing the upper part of a gaff sail from sagging away to leeward. The only more effective method is to rig a gaff vang*, which works well on a ketch or schooner, but is often found to be unleadable on a cutter.

Some gaffers have one topping lift*, others two. Two is preferable on a boat with a heavy boom so that you will always be able to 'top up' on the weather side. The lift does not then interfere with what you are trying to do with the sail. This cutter has simple purchases for her topping lifts, though many vessels of her size would opt for something more powerful.

The topsail(e) is hoisted on a single yard. The halyard is attached to this while the tack of the sail is bent to a downhaul. This keeps the luff of the sail straight. The cantilever effect pulls the yard upright. Had the boat been a little larger, she would have required a whip* on the topsail halyard to help with the weight of the yard. The downhaul has a purchase at its lower end.

The topsail sheet is organised in the same way as on any cutter. It passes first through a cheek block* on the outboard end of the gaff, then to the foot of the mast via a block, or bullseye*, which hangs from the gaff jaws. It is quite normal for a 40-footer to have no form of purchase on the topsail sheet, although the reason for this is convenience rather than that none is needed. If you think about what the sheet must do as the sail is hoisted and lowered, you'll see that there is no possibility of its carrying a permanently rigged tackle. The pull on the sheet can be substantial, but if you can't manage to set it up, it can always be dealt with by clapping on a handy billy*.

That concludes our whistle-stop tour of a well-organised basic cutter. She has what she needs in the way of running and standing rigging, and not a foot more. Some gaff sailors of today glory in the amount of rope which can be draped aloft, but this, I submit, is a poor approach to the business. Everything above the waterline creates wind resistance which diminishes the boat's weatherliness. Even a burgee halyard applies a significant pull in a strong breeze. Each item in the rig, and every yard of cordage must be there for a very good reason, otherwise it is counter-productive. The 'gear freak' will never win an old gaffer's race, and when he goes cruising he will find his vessel frustratingly slow to windward.

If this seems an extreme point of view, take a look at a Falmouth oyster dredger, working boat and racing yacht combined. Her rig is so slick, the wind blows straight through it until she spreads her canvas. Then she climbs upwind so tightly you'd think she had her engine running, if nobody had told you she does not have one.

A Falmouth working boat.

27

CHAPTER III

MASTS AND SPARS

In the past, a rig had to be made very heavy by today's standards to be sure it would be strong enough. If you put the rig from the Colin Archer in the previous chapter into a 40ft light displacement cruiser, it would probably lay her flat if she were caught beam-on by a sharp squall. This, of course, does not happen to the right boat for the rig. Indeed, almost the contrary is the case, because designers and builders of such vessels constructed hulls with the power and the displacement to cope easily with the capsizing effect of all that mass aloft. Whilst saving weight up there is always worthwhile, we don't have to worry over-much about saving a pound or two at the hounds* if we have a traditional boat which still sails to her original specification. All these calculations have been done for us, by men working without computers, who understood far better than we do the need to allow a great margin for safety.

MASTS

There are two distinct types of mast for gaff-rigged craft: the pole mast, and the mast which carries a fidded topmast*. Traditionally, both were of solid construction and, unless rigged in a tabernacle specifically for easy lowering, were stepped on the keel. The added security of this arrangement has been proved time and again to be well worth the puny trade-offs of lost accommodation space and leaks at the partners, which should never be a problem in any case, if the mast coat is in good condition.

A simple mast for a basic gaff rig is fairly short. It carries its upper throat halyard block somewhere in the vicinity of the hounds, and its peak blocks ranged on the short extension. Masts like this do not usually carry a topsail. They are sometimes seen on fishing smacks and small craft, or as the foremast on a 'bald-headed' schooner. It would be unusual for such a spar to bear any staying above the hounds.

The fidded topmast arrangement is an obvious development from the form described above. The hounds and masthead fittings are modified so that a slender topmast can slide through them forward of the main spar. When fully hoisted, it is held in place in the lower fitting by a fid. The presence of the topmast does not affect the arrangements for the lower sails, it merely supplies a convenient and elegant way of increasing sail area. A topsail and a jib topsail can be set from it.

A topmast is lifted into position by means of a heel-rope. In its simplest form, the rope is dead-ended at one side of the mast cap of the lower spar, led down through the lower topmast housing, around a sheave in the heel of the topmast, back up to the other side of the mast cap, around a turning block and thence to the deck. It is usually necessary to station a hand at the mast cap to guide the topmast through its fittings in the early stages of the hoist, then to shove home the fid at the end. As with all such operations, greasing the various apertures with tallow works miracles for easing the job as well as protecting the varnish.

If your boat does not have a topmast heel-rope, or even the blocks to carry one, the spar can usually be sent aloft by rigging the jib halyard as a temporary expedient. Its blocks are often at about the right height to work perfectly. Nowadays, when topmasts are only rarely lowered during the season, such a compromise makes good sense. Windage aloft is cut down, and the weight of a rope is saved.

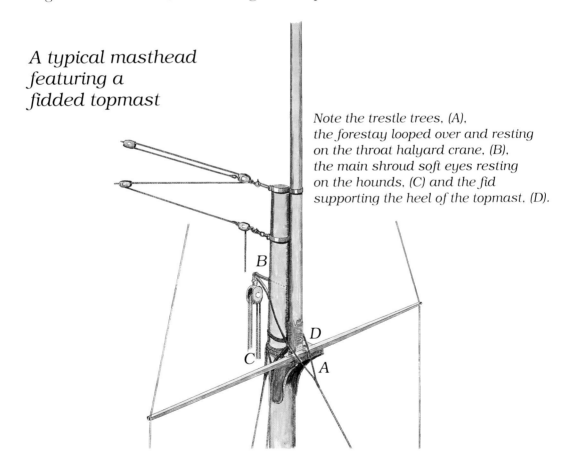

A typical masthead featuring a fidded topmast

Note the trestle trees, (A), the forestay looped over and resting on the throat halyard crane, (B), the main shroud soft eyes resting on the hounds, (C) and the fid supporting the heel of the topmast, (D).

Masts with topmasts almost invariably carry spreaders and a separate set of shrouds for the topmast itself. This will also have its own forestay to the bowsprit end as well as, in certain cases, a pair of running backstays known as 'preventers'. These latter are vital if a jib topsail is to be carried in any but the lightest of airs. The pilot cutters of the Bristol Channel used short topmasts which were often unstayed but for a forestay. So many of these went over the side that by 1910 most new cutters were opting for ultra-modern pole masts. These went some way towards offering the best of both worlds.

The pole mast stands lower than the topmast on an equivalent boat, but it is considerably longer than the basic spar. The extra length is all above the hounds. Some pole masts are tall enough to set a topsail without a yard to extend its luff, though most are not. The usual set-up is a short yard on the upper half of the topsail, though in some smaller vessels the yard may run from the head of the sail almost to the tack.

An unexpected advantage of a pole mast is that the jib halyard blocks (often cheek blocks) can be hung higher than would otherwise be the case. This makes for a jib luff closer to the vertical, which aids the cause of pointing to windward. The peak halyard blocks can be carried higher up as well, increasing the mechanical advantage of the halyards, reducing strains, and giving the crew an easier time when hoisting sail.

Pole masts are sometimes unstayed above the hounds, but the mast cap is more usually supported by a pair of light shrouds which may be assisted by spreaders. As with a topmast, an extra forestay is always rigged from the head of the pole mast to the bowsprit end, otherwise the aft pull of the topsail would cause some extremely eccentric bending.

In the last days of the gaff-rigged racing yacht, some of the big cutters sported an extended pole mast which was as tall as a topmast would have been. By this time, Bermudan rig was in existence and had gone part of the way to solving the staying problems which this entailed. The arrangement was convenient but short-lived, because within a year or two boats thus fitted out had either been pensioned off or fully converted to Bermudan rig, as was the King's cutter, *Britannia*. The Laurent Giles designed cruising yacht *Dyarchy* followed this general principle in the 1930s. Her rig proved reliable, handsome, and I can personally testify to its upwind capabilities. Nevertheless, her innovative features were largely left on the shelf by the Bermudan tide.

BOWSPRITS

As we have already seen, the bowsprit of a sloop is a structural part of the rig, because the main forestay is set up to its outboard end. For this reason, bowsprits on sloops are generally not over-long. They are also stout and strongly stayed.

Classically, a bowsprit is supported laterally by shrouds stretched between the cranse iron* and the shoulders of the vessel, where they are attached to chain plates somewhere around deck level. If spreaders are necessary, they are called 'whiskers' for obvious reasons. The spar is held down against the pull of jib or staysail by means of a

Forestaying arrangements typical of a working cutter

Note that the main forestay passes through a hole in the stemhead and is set up with a lanyard on the deck. Note also the bobstay tackle and tricing line for clearing the stay out of the way when anchoring or mooring.

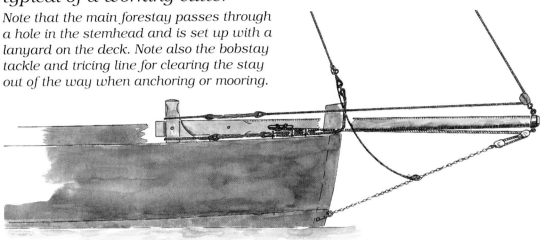

bobstay, which can be either wire, chain, or a solid bar tightened up with a rigging screw. The lower bobstay fitting is bolted through the stem in the vicinity of the waterline. At its upper end, the stay is attached to the lower lug of the cranse iron.

In a cutter, the staying of the bowsprit can be more casual, because unlike the sloop, the cutter does not rely on the bowsprit for mast support; or at least, not to any vital extent. The traditional cutter would run her bowsprit in and out by means of a heel-rope, in a similar way to a topmast. Many even reefed them in order that the end should coincide with the tack of each of their selection of jibs. Where this was done regularly, the spar was frequently innocent of any staying at all, and many an 80ft sailing trawler went to sea without a bobstay. Such vessels missed out in sailing efficiency, because it was impossible to achieve a really tight jib luff against a bowsprit that poked further and further skyward as her crew heaved up the halyards. Even so, it was felt that having shrouds and bobstay set up with tackles was more trouble than it was worth. Not everyone thought like this, however, and in other types which ran their 'sprits in and out, adjustable standing rigging was the order of the day.

When a fully rigged bowsprit is being run out, remember to make certain that all your shroud and bobstay tackles are thoroughly overhauled. So long as this has been taken care of, and the gammon iron* and bitts* are well greased, the spar will render easily, but woe betide the hapless mariner who stands on the fall of the bobstay purchase. It takes surprisingly little effort for the tail of a powerful tackle to hold up the combined efforts of two or three men.

Nowadays, most cutters carry their bowsprits permanently extended, even if the boat originally ran it in. Where this is the case, it usually makes sense to rig the spar with shrouds and a bobstay. The shrouds are the less important of the two, but even if

31

the spar is stout enough to be safe without them, they are a great psychological boost for the skipper. I've spent hours peering at bowsprits bending away to leeward, convincing myself that they wouldn't break. They very rarely have, which probably proves that I am an inveterate worrier. The bobstay, on the other hand, is a winner every time, and it never causes any trouble, particularly if rigged as it would have been when the spar was instantly retrievable.

The ideal form is to have a chain for about three quarters of the length of the stay. The final section just below the bowsprit end is taken up with a tackle whose fall is led back to the deck. This is let off and overhauled in harbour so that the bobstay can be triced up clear of the anchor cable or mooring by means of a light line attached halfway along its length. Tricing the bobstay gives anyone sleeping up forward a quiet night, which they'll deserve after a day of heaving your jibs up and down.

Such an arrangement would not, of course, be workable on a sloop, but why all cutters do not use it is a mystery.

A fine bowsprit, working well in a hard breeze.

GAFFS

Gaffs on working craft were usually solid, grown spars. On yachts they became hollow as soon as effective glues were available. A hollow spar can be immensely strong, and the saving in weight is so substantial that even a gaffer can benefit from it so high up the mast.

We have already considered the positioning of the topsail sheet blocks on most gaffs (Chapter II), but we have not noted that in days of yore they were usually on the port side. The only reason I can offer for this, other than a long-standing fashion, is that a jib-headed topsail* at least will always come down without a struggle with the wind forward of the beam, so long as it is on the lee side of the mainsail. Obviously, the boat is less manoeuvrable while executing her 'topsail drop'. If any chance should arise of a collision with another craft, it would be preferable for the compromised boat

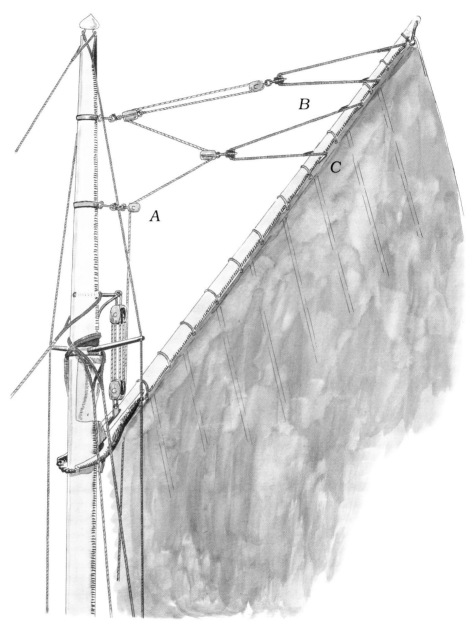

The masthead of a pole-masted cutter

(Headsail gear omitted for clarity.)
Note shroud soft eyes and forestay. Lower peak halyard block is pitched aft by a link of chain at the mast to allow it to clear throat crane when tacking/gybing,(A). Note gaff spans well outboard, (B) and thumb cleats, (C), all inboard of splices.

to be on the starboard tack. Hence, topsails were always set on the port side for preference. (see Chapter VII for more on this subject)

One comes across sundry arrangements for attaching peak halyard blocks to gaffs. The span* system is certainly the kindest, but photographs of different vessels from around the Atlantic basin show that in the past it was a case of 'anything goes'. The one thing they all had in common was that the weight was taken in various locations on the gaff, spreading the load, and reducing the chances of springing the spar.

The throat halyard must be attached to the gaff so that when the angle of the spar is changed by peaking up, no strain is caused anywhere. There are almost as many ways of achieving this as there were spar-makers. Most work adequately, but it is important that the halyard, its block, and the luff of the sail all remain 'in column', no matter what may betide. Certain rigs designed recently have ignored this lesson of history with resulting strains and damage to sails.

When the sail is hoisted, the gaff is under compression, which holds it against the mast. In low-tech working craft this state of affairs is expedited by employing leathered gaff jaws. These consist of a grown hardwood extension on either side of the gaff which

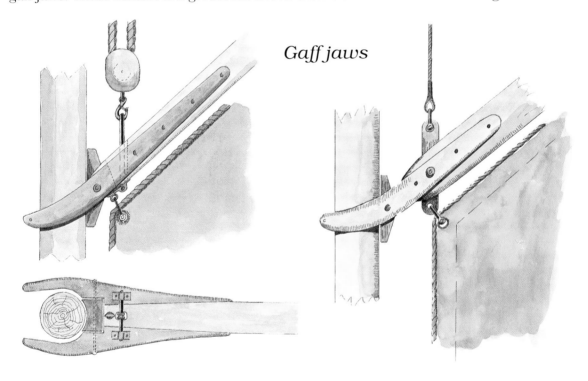

Gaff jaws

There are numerous effective ways of arranging the throat end of a gaff. It is important that blocks and sail luff more or less line up with the sail hoisted.

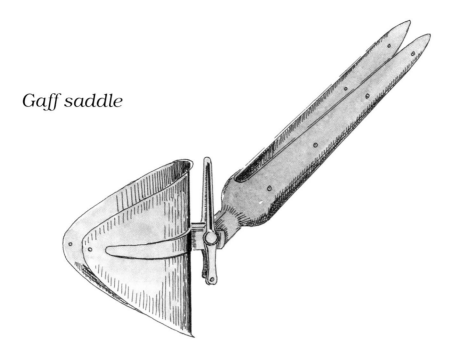

Gaff saddle

slides loosely on the mast as though the two pieces of wood were the prongs of a pitchfork. The actual compression is borne by a chock of leathered wood, shaped on its forward side to fit the mast radius, fastened into the gaff jaws on a single bolt which allows it to swivel at will. In the UK this block is called the tumbler; in the US it is known as the chip, and here it is often flat in its forward section, rather than having an inside radius.

A more modern method of coping with the inboard end of the gaff is to use a metal 'saddle', made up to fit the radius of the mast. The saddle supplies the sideways support of gaff jaws and the compression resistance of a tumbler all in one. Like gaff jaws, a saddle is leathered, and is retained around the forward side of the mast with a lanyard bearing a number of parrel balls, just in case the peak halyards are let go while the throat is still up. If this is done under control, as sometimes it may be, no harm befalls, but if it occurs at the run due to an accident or a piece of incompetence, the gaff 'capsizes' and the compression disappears. The only thing then retaining the gaff on the mast will be the parrel lanyard.

All gaff jaws and saddles must be kept greased in order to protect them, the mast, and the crew's nerves. The 'graunching' of a dry gaff saddle creaking in protest will be projected through the ship by the sounding board of the mast, especially when she is reaching in choppy water and light winds. Tallow has still not been surpassed as a general purpose grease for lubricating leatherwork. It's clean, it smells like sheep, which are far sweeter than most animals, including hardworking humans, and it is available from all family butchers.

BOOMS

It is absolutely pointless to put a light-weight boom on a gaffer. Unless the boom is made of aluminium and the whole rig is so light it might as well have been Bermudan, you are unlikely to be able to rig an effective kicking strap or vang on a gaffer of over 30ft. The only thing which will keep the boom down once the sheet is eased is its own mass, and a fine, meaty spar will do this very effectively indeed.

There is, therefore, no advantage in specifying a hollow boom, unless the vessel is so large either that the spar must be built up in order to achieve the desired length, or that a solid length of timber would be simply too heavy to handle under any circumstances. A grown spar will do the job better and more cheaply. Granted, it will represent some additional weight permanently stationed above the boat's centre of gravity, but as we have already noted, any heavy displacement craft with gaff rig has almost certainly been designed to cope easily with that sort of thing. We have also remarked that a light displacement gaffer would be virtually a contradiction in terms, so heavy booms are almost invariably good news. I've sailed with both, and I haven't the slightest doubt about this.

If a boom is rigged for conventional reefing, it should ideally be thinner at the goose-neck end, then fill out halfway along, where it is most likely to be whipped around by compression forces coming inboard from the clew of the mainsail. At its outboard extremity it will carry the reef combs, one on either side. These long, hardwood fittings are bolted through the boom. They supply the wherewithal for leading the reefing pendants forward from the sail to the reefing tackle or winch.

Usually reefing combs are fitted with a hole on one side paired with a sheave on the other, repeated for however many reefs are available. In this way, one end of the pendant is dead-ended by a stopper knot beneath the hole. It is then led up through the reef cringle, on through the sheave, and thence to the power source for heaving it down. This method has the advantage of giving a 2:1 multiple factor (minus the considerable frictional losses) to be applied to whatever the reefing tackle or winch is delivering.

In case this sounds like an unmitigated source of happiness, there is another aspect to be considered. If the sheave is on the lee side of the sail, the cloth below the reef cringle will tend to be drawn into it by the pendant. This is good for neither the canvas nor the blood pressure of the poor souls trying to pull down the reef. So long as the sheave is on the windward side, the sail will blow away from it and this will never happen. On balance, then, it seems better to have sheaves on both sides of the comb. It will then always be possible to pull that side of the pendant which is to windward, after first dead-ending the other with a quick figure-of-eight knot.

If the boom is of the roller-reefing type, the mainsheet will be attached to the outboard end at a swivel, which also supplies a home for the topping lifts. Otherwise, the sheet block, or blocks, will probably be on a strop which, like a gaff span, serves to spread the load and allow them full freedom of movement.

There is no difference between the goose-neck of a gaffer and any other vessel, except that it must be particularly robust to bear the weight of the boom. A roller-

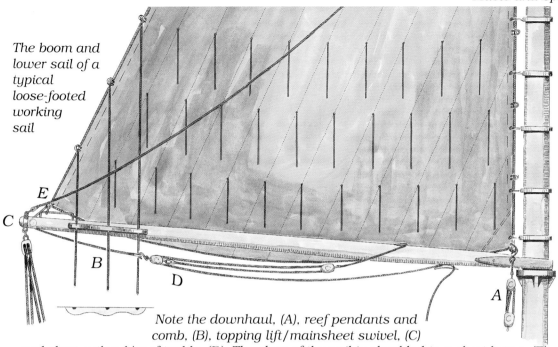

The boom and lower sail of a typical loose-footed working sail

E

C

B

D

A

Note the downhaul, (A), reef pendants and comb, (B), topping lift/mainsheet swivel, (C) and clew outhaul/reef tackle, (D). The clew of the sail is shackled to a short horse, (E).

reefing boom will have the patent mechanism just outboard of the goose-neck. While there are a number of types of gear which may be regularly encountered, most are over-engineered, heavy, and completely reliable as a result.

Because of their comparatively vertical leeches, gaff sails roller reef better than their three-cornered counterparts. This is particularly so on the mainsail of a ketch, or a schooner foresail (where the arrangement is rarely seen), because the leech and luff are almost parallel. If a cutter or sloop is rigged with roller reefing, the angle of her mainsail leech will cause her boom to droop after a few rolls, unless the outboard end of the spar is fatter than the inboard end. If the boom appears unsuitable by virtue of being parallel sided, amends can sometimes be made by screwing gently tapered battens along the outboard half of the boom's length, with their thick ends aft.

Certain types of gaff-rigged craft have always sailed without booms. These do not all employ permanently standing gaffs, though many take full advantage of the potential their boomlessness offers for brailing up the sail. The Bawley of the east coast of England enjoys a rig that has been perfected in this way.

Some schooners (including the *America* in her heyday) sport an overlapping foresail which must perforce be boomless. For most of us, however, whether our mainsails are laced to it, or set from it loose-footed with only tack and clew attached, the boom is a part of our everyday lives. In the majority of gaff-rigged craft, it is long and heavy. For obvious reasons, it pays to get into the habit of always considering boom and topping lift in the same thought-process. If you train yourself to 'think topping lift', you'll save skulls, sails, and deck joinery from many a terminal crack-up.

CHAPTER IV

STANDING RIGGING

It is easy to imagine that in order to perform well and be secure, a rig must be set up bar-taut. This idea stems from the influence of modern craft, where high technology encourages tensions to be so great that the lee rigging hardly sags at all, even in a strong breeze. When it comes to traditional craft, however, the proposition is not entirely true. On the one hand, if standing rigging is to work properly it seems only reasonable that it should keep the mast as upright as possible, yet when one travels in places where boats still work under sail, it is a surprise to note how well some vessels eat up to windward under outrageously baggy sails, and masts which bend to the wind like pines in a forest.

We Westerners have much to learn from the crews of these primitive boats. They have not been brought up on a diet of media babble about heroes who 'conquer the Atlantic'. Like our own forebears, such sailors do not fight the sea and the wind. They work with them, giving a little here, taking what they may there, and holding onto what ground they can when conditions become too severe to continue. They arrive at their destination as a result of an honourable compromise with the elements which allows their low-stressed ships to give service for decades.

While the northern gaff rig is a much tighter affair than the amazing stick-and-string contraptions which power the Brazilian saveiro or the West Indian sailing lighter, it is still essentially a give-and-take arrangement. Masts, spars and standing rigging are not so much engineered as created, so that on the whole, it is a work of art rather than science. If we approach it as such, we will be alive to its benefits and will not be disappointed by its shortcomings.

The standing rigging which supports the mast on a gaff-rigged vessel is simple in design, robust in structure and reliable in operation. In its classical forms there are none of the patent terminals which can cause problems in stainless steel and aluminium rigs. Everything is worked by hand, and, unless your boat uses rigging screws, the most finely engineered component is likely to be a galvanised shackle.

Traditionally, shrouds have loops in their upper ends. They are passed over the masthead and slid down the spar until they settle on the bolsters. These short wooden 'sleepers' rest on hardwood cheeks which are let into the mast and through-bolted for additional security. Together with the bolsters, the cheeks make up the hounds of the mast.

Forestays are looped over the masthead in a similar manner, but they are often not carried as far down as the hounds. In many boats the forestay sits on the upper surface of the throat halyard crane*, while sometimes a separate iron thumb cleat is provided for it to rest upon. Backstay pendants are also lowered over the masthead and snugged down at the hounds.

The loops of the masthead rigging of a pole mast, or the forestay, shrouds (sometimes called 'backstays), and preventers (where fitted) of the topmast, usually rest on a shoulder cut around the masthead a few inches below the truck*.

Some rigs do not have loops on the upper ends of their shrouds and stays, preferring a hard-eye which is shackled to a tang on the relevant mast band. These are a driven fit, hammered down onto the taper of the spar. Often they are further secured in place by a shoulder, or an iron thumb cleat let into the mast and screwed in position. It is by no means uncommon for a rig to carry its main shrouds and forestay in looped form, with everything else shackled on.

Loops are made with a circumference $1\frac{1}{2}$ times that of the mast at the hounds, if that is where they are to sit. Loops made to rest on a masthead shoulder should be $1\frac{1}{4}$ times the circumference. These clearances give them enough slack for manoeuvre, but not so much that they are in danger of slipping below their allotted place.

If you are making up new rigging, the best plan is to measure the distance from the bolster to the chain plate* for each shroud, with the mast in the boat and the old rigging set up. If the boat has never been rigged, the measurement will have to be done by means of a plan. Just make sure that you note the distance to the chain plate concerned, and not directly down to the deck, otherwise the fore-and-aft 'spread' of the shrouds will bring your efforts to nought.

Once you have the overall length, subtract whatever the measurement will be between the upper and lower dead-eyes, or the length of the bottlescrew when almost fully extended. There is now a final adjustment to be made: you must decide what order the shrouds, backstays and forestay (if that too is to rest on the hounds) will be laid on the bolsters. The first shroud over the masthead is the length as measured, the next is the measured length plus twice the shroud diameter; four times the diameter is added to the third, six times to the fourth, and so on.

A single loop aloft is generally worked into a shroud by means of a handsplice. It is then parcelled with tarred canvas and served with marline. On a big boat where loadings will be heavy, leather will do this job better. If the loop is on a shroud which is one of a pair (e.g. the port or starboard main shrouds in a 35ft ketch), many people prefer to use one length of wire for both shrouds, with a wire seizing* joining the two parts together just below the bolster to form the loop. This makes for less wires piling up at the hounds, as well as saving a small amount of weight aloft. Unfortunately, it also means that if the seizing gives up the ghost, both shrouds on one side will slacken suddenly and may slip away altogether. The results could be expensive and inconvenient, but such an occurrence is exceedingly rare, so long as whoever works the seizing has his mind on the job.

If the lower end of a shroud is to be attached to a rigging screw or set up with a simple lanyard, the only tidy choice is to splice or swage in a hard-eye and shackle it on. Where the wire is passing round a dead-eye, however, it is just as easy to seize it back upon itself with a minimum of three racking seizings*. In both cases the work should be served with marline.

On a long-term basis, it is better to seize than to splice, because the process of splicing will degrade the galvanising on the wire. This is less important aloft where, in an ideal world at least, corrosive salt water will not be present in any quantity. The shrouds at deck-level, however, are constantly being soaked in sea-water if the boat is regularly sailed out in the open. The service of a splice is rarely as perfectly effective a form of waterproofing as we'd like, and so the rot creeps in.

SEIZINGS

Seizings can be in wire, or soft small stuff, but wire is always employed for standing rigging. The monel variety sold on handy little reels is beautiful to use, strong, and inert to corrosion. It is also expensive. At the other end of the cost scale, galvanised fencing wire has been successfully employed. If you choose this, however, it will need frequent black varnishing to keep the water out, as well as twice yearly inspections for rust. All seizings should be set up as tightly as you are able. The limiting factor is the strength of the wire or marline. So long as that does not break you are not overdoing it. Ideally, a seizing should be hove taut, turn by turn, with a seizing mallet. If you do not possess one, or have not acquired the necessary skills to use it, much can be achieved by the creative use of a proper marline spike.

The flat seizing

This is used for bringing two wires or lines together when both will be under equal loads, such as where shrouds are paired at the masthead. Here, the seizing is started by hitching the wire to one part of the pair. It is then passed round and round the two shrouds, pulling them together, until a dozen or so turns (13 for luck, some would say) have been laid on. The job is finished by taking the seizing wire around the seizing lengthways, and frapping the turns up hard. This is done twice, and each time the end is passed under the loop you are making. The result is a clove hitch. When you have hauled this up tight, you can snip the end off with a pair of pliers, and tidy up.

The racking seizing

This type of seizing is made to hold together two parts of a wire, where one part only will carry the load. A typical application is at the lower end of a shroud after it has been passed around a dead-eye. The first set of turns must number at least the 7 recommended by the Bible for critical counts, though a dozen is better. These are wound around and between the parts of the shroud in a 'figure-eight' configuration. The wire is then wound round and round back to the starting point, heaving up hard at every turn so that it beds down in between each part of the figures-of-eight. Finish the seizing by frapping, as with the flat seizing. If four or five of these are worked neatly into a shroud, it will never move, not even by an eighth of an inch.

THE ORDERLY MASTHEAD

The first shroud on the bolster is, by convention, always the starboard forward. It is followed by the port forward, the starboard aft, then the port aft. If there are three per side, the aftermost pair still goes on top. Any backstay pendants sit underneath everything, while the forestay, if it is to rest in the same cluster as the others rather than higher up, settles over the whole lot.

A similar order is followed for any cap-shrouds and forestay, or for a topmast forestay, 'backstays', and preventers.

FORESTAYS

There are two main ways of terminating the lower end of a gaffer's forestay. The first is with a hard-eye shackled to a rigging screw which is set up on the stemhead, or the bowsprit end if she is a sloop. Sophisticated cutter yachts may even carry the forestay fitting inboard of the stem. Older types, however, particularly if they have a straight stem, may bring the whole forestay inboard through the upper part of the stem, from forward to aft. The arrangement has the overriding advantage that most of the load of the forestay is carried by the stem itself, rather than some other fitting fastened to it. Because of the enormous friction created as the wire passes through the timber, only a modest proportion of the strain is transferred to the tensioning device, or its deck fitting.

When the stay has been led through the hole in the stem it is seized back on itself to form a hard-eye, then set up with a lanyard or rigging screw running aft to a strong point on the deck, the bitts for example. If you're feeling lazy, try bulldog grips* to replace the seizings. These are quick to use, as well as being reliable. They can also be readily removed, so that the lower end of the forestay can be withdrawn from its hiding place for inspection at annual refit time.

The last item is an important one. If a forestay is going to break, it will probably be here that the trouble starts. However well parcelled and served the portion hidden in the stem may be, it is vulnerable to the dreaded sea-water. This lodges in the hole, soaks the service and the wire inside, then takes a long time to drain away, if indeed it does so at all. Most of it will evaporate, leaving an ever-strengthening acid solution to nibble at the wire.

Replacing a forestay is expensive, but losing one is even more of a bankroll basher, so there must be no temptation to compromise. One excellent tip for getting the most out of the main length of the stay, while being in a position to sacrifice the vulnerable part, is this: the forestay is finished off immediately above the stemhead with a well-served hard-eye. This is then shackled to another hard-eye on the end of a short length of wire of similar diameter. The short length is now led through the hole in the stem and seized back on itself as if it were the forestay. It will certainly become suspect long before the stay itself. When it does, it can be easily and cheaply replaced.

A topmast forestay is frequently terminated at the bowsprit end with nothing more than a shackle. Such a stay is carefully measured, and relies upon the bobstay tackle or rigging screw to tension it. More often, its own rigging screw will be fitted between its lower end and the cranse iron. On larger vessels the stay is sometimes fully adjustable, just as it might be for a reeving bowsprit. The favourite method of achieving this is to reeve the stay through a turning block at the bowsprit end, then back to the foredeck where it can be set up with a tackle or a lanyard. The time to heave it up tight is immediately before setting a topsail when close-hauled.

BACKSTAYS

While all the standing rigging of gaff masts is individual, it is never more so than in the case of backstays. Some boats may ignore their very invention, others would not go to sea without them. It is therefore utterly impossible to generalise.

The inherent problem with backstaying a gaffer is the gaff itself. You cannot have a standing backstay because it will stop the gaff from crossing the centre-line of the vessel. Any backstays must therefore be of the 'running' variety, whereby the weather backstay is always set up, with the leeward one let off.

This incurs a number of disadvantages:

— It involves your crew in an extra job when the boat tacks. If they aren't crowding the deck like sardines, they'll have enough work without it.

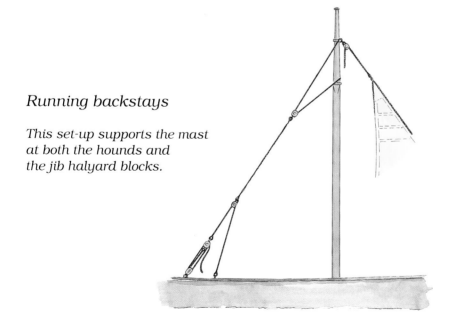

Running backstays

This set-up supports the mast at both the hounds and the jib halyard blocks.

— It has been said with justification that as soon as you put runners on a mast you make it vulnerable. Sooner or later, the boom will be gybed onto a made-up runner. If the spar is heavy, the gybe severe, and the preventer backstay is in the way, the topmast will take a trip to the ocean blue. Where the lower runner absorbs the brunt of the incident, you may be dismasted, or break your boom, or both.

— To set against these two unpleasantnesses is the fact that it is easier to achieve a tight headsail luff if the halyard can be pulled up in opposition to a running backstay.

The gaff-rigged racing yacht would certainly opt for runners. The working boat, unless she were racing, would equally surely have nothing to do with them. Even pilot cutters, the performance brigade of the working world, didn't have running backstays. However, lest anyone go off with the idea that to operate without backstays is merely a matter of chopping them down, it should be clearly understood that the working vessels which did not use them had a different deployment of shrouds to those yachts which did.

In a pole-masted English pilot cutter, the forward lower shrouds were in line with the mast, while the aft lowers spread out towards the quarter. The aftermost shrouds of the three main pairs were in reality a form of backstay. Their chain plates* were sited three or four feet abaft the forward ones, and the upper end of the shroud attached to the mast in the vicinity of the jib halyard blocks. This enabled the jib luff to be set up tight without tweaking the upper section of the mast forward at an impossible angle.

You might imagine that the position of these aft shrouds would prevent the boom being properly squared off downwind, with weather helm produced as a result, but in practice this is not the case. With the boom up against the aft shroud, the gaff

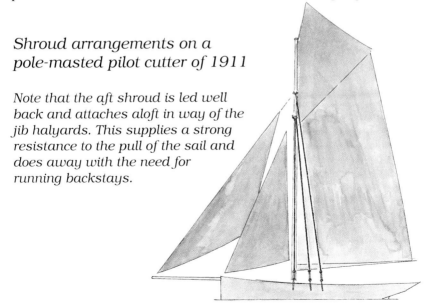

Shroud arrangements on a pole-masted pilot cutter of 1911

Note that the aft shroud is led well back and attaches aloft in way of the jib halyards. This supplies a strong resistance to the pull of the sail and does away with the need for running backstays.

generally twists off to an athwartships position. To square away any further would cause rolling problems.

The system is beautiful in its simplicity, and goes a long way towards solving the perennial problem of backstaying a gaffer.

We have seen how the pendant part of the backstay is generally looped around the mast at the hounds, but some rigs must perforce have their pendants shackled on aloft. On pole masts which require extra backstaying in way of the jib halyard blocks, the pendant may be a strop, with one end at the hounds, the other at the desired point. A block, or some other form of sliding device, is then fitted into the bight* of the pendant strop, with the true pendant passing down towards the deck from its becket*

About halfway between the hounds and the deck, the runner is attached to the pendant, usually by a block shackled to a hard-eye worked into its lower end. One end of the runner is shackled at the deck. The other is equipped with a tensioning device of some sort, whose power is doubled by the fact that it is effectively on the end of a whip, which gives a 2:1 purchase. On working vessels and older yachts, the tension was provided by a tackle, which would usually be of 4:1 power made up of two double blocks with a becket on the lower one. Yachts often preferred the 'Highfield Lever' principle, which is quick to operate on the wind. Most examples are made in such a way that it is easy to cast off the lee runner on a reach.

The other advantage of the Highfield Lever is that if everything has been measured correctly, and your mainsail is not cut over-full, you have only to set up the lever on the new tack and throw off the old one, to have the pendant clear the lee side of the sail. This can often be done from the cockpit of a small craft. Once you have the knack of the timing, the job can be successfully executed with remarkably little fuss.

Tricing lines are often fitted from a small block on the aft shrouds to the bight of the runner. Hauling down on this draws the wire away from the sail when the backstay is let off on the lee side, but never forget to let the line off before trying to whack over the Highfield Lever. If you manage it, that'll be the last you see of your tricing block.

While topmast shrouds are officially known as backstays, it is the preventers which really stop the topmast falling over the bows when the Yankee is pulling like crazy on a broad reach. Preventers are frequently set up with a 4:1 purchase, rigged as far aft as convenient, generally on the quarter. You don't have to make up your preventers every time you are using the topmast. They are usually only required when you are well off the wind and driving hard, but a glance up the mast from the goose-neck will remove any ambiguity from your mind. Mast movements always appear more dramatic when looking directly aloft up the shaft of the spar, and many's the time I've strolled casually forward to take a peep, then broken every rule in the sailor's book by galloping aft to the preventer tackle. Like everything else on a gaffer, a preventer is more effective if set up before the load comes on. The moral must therefore be, 'if in doubt, set it up,' but never, never, gybe onto it all standing.

SETTING UP THE RIG

The question of how tight to set up a gaff rig will be the subject of gang murders for as long as there are oil lamps to swing and ale to be drunk. Before the introduction of wire rope, rigs used to be kept on the slack side because hemp cordage, even if heavily tarred, stretched considerably. It also shrank, and if you really whacked it on hard on a hot dry day, it could find itself under serious strain if the next night turned out cold and rainy.

By 1880, however, that prolific commentator Dixon Kemp was remarking that there was nothing to be gained from slack rigging. On the face of things, it does seem that since the rigging is there to stop the mast from falling down, it may as well do it from the outset of a breeze, rather than wait until the spar is leaning over from the vertical.

Bearing this in mind, as well as what was said about primitive vessels at the beginning of this chapter, it will be clear that reason and moderation supply the answers when setting up a rig, particularly if it is equipped with the all-powerful rigging screw. I have seen evidence of production fibreglass boats and their rigs being strained by over-indulgence with a 3ft tommy bar. Imagine what a butcher thus armed could do to a 70-year-old wooden yacht. Fortunately, it is nigh on impossible to over-tighten a lanyard if you are using only the throat halyard and its purchase for power.

On any rig, it is a good plan to address the shrouds from the bottom of 'the stack' upwards, once the mast has been positioned vertically with its wedges. This means that you begin with the starboard forward, and move on to the port forward, etc. If both pairs of shrouds are doubled back and seized at the hounds, you'll have to compromise here, but commonsense will prevail.

As soon as the mast is held upright by one shroud a side, it makes sense to put some tension on the main forestay. If this passes through the stem there will be a limit to what you can get, even if it has a rigging screw, because of the friction. Just take the kinks out of it, and leave the aft shrouds to do the job properly. On most craft this works very well, though if the forestay has its own rigging screw, adjustments can still be made at the end. Don't forget that if you have running backstays, they will complete the forestay tensioning when you throw the levers.

Keep checking that the mast is in column as you work on the shrouds. Sight from aft, from forward and from the goose-neck. If in doubt, use the topsail halyard as a 'plumb bob'. If this isn't convenient, use it as a measuring device by dropping it first to one rail then the other. Are both sides of the ship an equal distance from the top of the mast?

Yes? then carry on.

No? Hmmm.

Topmast backstays (shrouds) present no problems, while any tension you pull into the outer forestay will tweak the top-masthead towards the bows. Whether you like this look or not is a question both of fashion and the way your sails are cut. Topmasts on the east coast of England are bent well forward, while in France and the USA the 'in column' effect is generally preferred.

Setting up dead-eyes and lanyards

This is far less trouble than it might appear to the unenlightened. The first requirement is 'small ropes and big holes'. If your boat is a pensioner and has her original dead-eyes, this is easy to follow, because modern rope is far stronger than the Italian hemp of old. A lanyard can therefore be measurably thinner than its predecessor, and since the holes probably worked adequately in those days, any change can only make things even easier.

If you have a new boat, or new dead-eyes, don't be mean about drilling the holes. There are no sheaves in them, and you want the lanyards to render smoothly. The holes should be sweetly chamfered in the direction the lanyard will follow, and they must be well greased with tallow just before use. If you don't grease the dead-eyes you may as well stay at home.

Reeve up the dead-eyes with the stopper knots at the top, 'forward to starboard, aft to port, inside on both sides' (anyone sailing on my boat can remember this, because the maxim also applies to the heads compartments). Beginning with the starboard lanyard, make a small bowline in the end and hook on the lower throat halyard block. Heave up the halyard, finishing off with the purchase if necessary, until you are satisfied with the tension.

Now comes the clever bit. Make fast the halyard and bring out your lanyard wedge. This is a miniature hardwood wedge, scalloped out on one side to fit your lanyard, and convex on the other to fit the hole in the dead-eye. Using a small hammer, tap the wedge gently from the inboard side into the last hole that the lanyard is leaving before it attaches to the halyard block. As you let off the halyard the wedge will be drawn into the hole by the tension on the lanyard, but it will only move about a quarter of an inch before it locks the system up. Now you can untie your bowline and cow-hitch the end of the lanyard either around the top of the dead-eye inside the shroud loop, or around the bottom end of the shroud itself, just before it divides to form the loop.

Once the tail of the lanyard is secure, tap the wedge out sideways with your hammer and proceed to the next shroud. You can deal with six in an hour when you're into the swing of things. After you've done the lot and you're satisfied that all the shrouds are taking an even share of the pull and that the forestay has come up tight enough, seize the lanyard tails down to their own falls with a short length of marline, leaving the cow hitches undisturbed.

It is extremely unwise to tighten lanyards by taking up the slack on the lee side while under way. If you can't work out why, don't ever buy a wooden boat.

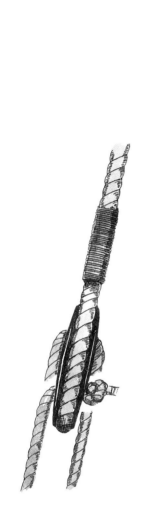

CHAPTER V

RUNNING GEAR

THE TACKLE

The only unassisted tackle left on a modern yacht of any size is the mainsheet. Even the fall of the kicking strap is often led aft to the multi-purpose coach-roof winch with its bank of stoppers. On craft over 40ft, it is commonplace to lead the tail of the mainsheet itself to a winch of its own. From this, the sailors of today with no knowledge of history could be forgiven for concluding that the tackle really isn't much use as a source of power. 'No guts in it,' they might be heard muttering. 'Looks pretty enough, but for a real pull give me a two-speed, top action, self-tailing wonder-grinder.'

They couldn't be more wrong. 90-ton fishing ketches were sailed without winches, though it could be argued that they were always heavily crewed. Even short-handed, however, working boats were managed easily with tackle assistance alone. A Bristol Channel Pilot Cutter with an 800 sq ft mainsail was sailed by two men through the worst gales of winter. One of them was often little more than a boy. It was all done with tackles and experience.

Many gaff-rigged craft are now equipped with winches for some of the everyday jobs. Often the arrangement is successful, but by no means always. Headsail sheets are readily handled by winches, for example, but only if the drums are conveniently sited. There are few abominations like a winch placed so that it is impossible to throw one's weight at it. The modern yacht has her cockpit designed around her sheet winches, and unless this is done with a gaffer, the system is unlikely to succeed. A winch may boast a nominal 30:1 power in the handbook, but if you can't get near it to give it your all, it won't deliver anything approaching that. The same is true for a tackle, and if the fall of your staysail sheet purchase is jammed between the cockpit coaming and the toerail, with a guard-rail and dodger thrown in to skin the knuckles, you'll end up with a baggy sail and a double rupture. Generally speaking, though, a well-positioned, powerful tackle is an effective piece of kit. It is also entirely understandable to the non-mechanical mind. It is easily rigged, and it almost never fails.

A classic double-ended mainsheet

Note buffer, or jiber, on the central block at the deck.
The velocity ratio of the arrangement is 5:1, because one end of the mainsheet is always made fast.

The power of a tackle is theoretically the number of parts of rope at the moving block, as opposed to the standing block. On a mainsheet which has a double block and becket at the boom end, with a double block running beneath on a horse, the moving block would be the upper one, and the nominal power 5:1. This value is also called the Velocity Ratio of the tackle, because the hauling end is moving at five times the rate of the moving block. The mainsheet mentioned above is rove to advantage. If the tackle were turned upside down so that the final pull came upwards off the bottom block, the moving block would have only four parts of the rope. That would be the nominal power of the system, and the tackle would be rove to disadvantage.

If one tackle is rigged so that it pulls on the fall of another, as in the case of a permanently rigged purchase on the standing part of a double-ended halyard, the power of the two systems will be multiplied, rather than added together.

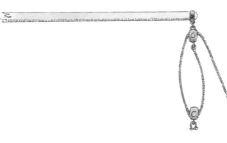

A 3:1 purchase rove to advantage as a mainsheet. Velocity ratio 3:1

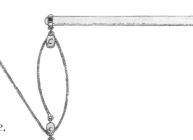

The same tackle rove to disadvantage. Velocity ratio 2:1

Frictional losses diminish the mechanical advantage of any tackle. They arise from two sources: the bearing surfaces where the sheaves turn on the pins, and the bending of the rope around the sheaves. Plenty of grease minimises the first of these. The second is best dealt with on the 'small ropes big sheaves' principle. A polyester rope that is not sun-degraded is beautifully soft compared with a length of wet manila, so if you rig with modern fibres, you will ease your work-load dramatically.

The more sheaves in a tackle, the greater the power loss. The mechanical advantage of the mainsheet described on the previous page would be around 3¾ if rove to advantage, and 2½ rove to disadvantage.

The upper block, or blocks, of a double-ended halyard will always have one sheave working as a becket, no matter which end is being pulled. It is the lower, moving block which defines the power of the basic halyard, and the upper block of the purchase which decides what the multiple factor will be. Suppose you have a throat halyard whose block on the gaff is a double. The mast block is a treble, and the purchase is a single block and becket at the deck with a double block on the end of the standing part of the halyard. The purchase has a velocity ratio of 4:1. So does the halyard. The velocity ratio of the whole system is therefore 16:1. So much is lost in friction that by the time you come to swing on the end of the purchase on a nasty night, the mechanical advantage will probably be down to ten or so.

When compared with the extravagant claims of a modern winch, an achievable power of 10:1 may not sound very impressive. In real life, however, what you are getting is, at the very least, ten times the gross body weight of the person pulling it. A 16-stone man can exert a ton with no more effort than tailing on and lifting his feet off the deck. An educated 8 stone woman who knows how to swig a rope on a belaying pin can probably do nearly as well without so much as raising her heart rate.

LEADS

There are so many ropes in even the best organised gaffer that good leads are essential if the whole show is to work properly. A bad lead will soon either make a job hard work, or generate a chafe problem. It will also be an offence to the eye.

The worst area for chafe aloft is usually in the vicinity of the hounds. Halyard falls have a way of becoming nipped by the gaff or the gaff jaws. There, they rub against the aft shrouds or the backstays until they part or are consigned to the skip. This latter form of demise is infuriating because the rope invariably chafes in the middle, which renders it useless and irreparable. You can always cut it up and use it for reefing pendants, sail ties, or even headsail sheets, but all of these are an ignominious end for a fine peak halyard or a topsail sheet.

One answer to distress of this nature is to hold the bight of the halyard away from the danger area by passing it through a bullseye seized to a shroud. If no bullseyes are to be had, a short length of plastic hose, painted black or taped round to ease its eyesore potential, can usually be 'lost' at the hounds. Fairleading the halyard fall through this should solve its problems.

The chafing of a sail caused by continual rubbing against a backstay or topping lift can only really be dealt with by rigging baggywrinkle* on the offending rope or wire. This should be regarded as a last ditch solution. A generous helping of baggywrinkle creates as much windage as the door of an outside toilet. Try opening one of those against a gale of wind and you'll realise why working vessels and gentlemen's yachts in the golden years of gaff used such chafing gear as little as possible.

With the exception of throat and peak, all the other halyards can be led in any way that suits the boat. Throat was, and still is, always to starboard unless there is an excellent reason to the contrary. When hove-to in order to reef the main, a seaman wanted to be on starboard tack so as to make the most of his collision rights. He also wanted to be working on the uphill side of the deck to keep his feet dry. Since many gaffers can tuck in two reefs before it becomes necessary to make more than minor adjustments to the peak halyard, it was sensible to keep the throat to starboard and the peak to port. If a boat is small enough for one person to pull both halyards at once, which is generally the case below about 35ft, both can be led to starboard.

By the same logic, if there is only one topping lift, it should be led down to the starboard side.

Topsail sheets belay at, or very near, the mast; on small vessels, they may be made fast on the inboard end of the boom itself alongside ensign halyards from the peak of the gaff.

Jib clews are sometimes rigged with a short pendant and a bullseye. A whip purchase is then rove through the bullseye to supply 2:1 power assistance. One end of this whip is made fast somewhere on the forward rail. After leading up through the bullseye, the hauling end is brought aft through a deck fairlead. The hauling part can have its purchase beefed up by rigging a further whip to its end, substantially abaft the fairlead. Alternatively, it may be led to a winch. Neither is necessary, however, on a well-sailed vessel of under 35ft.

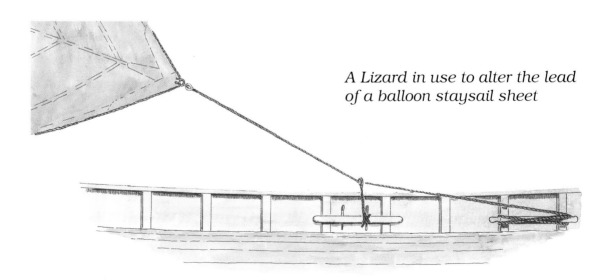

A Lizard in use to alter the lead of a balloon staysail sheet

51

The drawback of this rig is that the bullseyes frequently foul up on the forestay when short-tacking; they have also been known to cause broken heads amongst the foredeck hands. This can be avoided by attaching a pair of single-part sheets to the clew of the sail, instead of the bullseyes. These are led aft via the deck fairleads to whip purchases on either side. The whip is minimum equipment for power, but it can work on the jib in craft up to 50ft, so long as the helmsman is sympathetic to the creaking muscles of the crew.

The purchase for a simple staysail sheet is often rigged in the way just described for a jib. The only difference is in the power of the tackle. Unlike a jib, the staysail must be sheeted board flat when close-hauled in a hard breeze. 3:1 is therefore the required purchase up to 50ft — but it must be a genuine 3:1. It needs big blocks, with ropes that are small enough to render perfectly, but thick enough to handle comfortably. The fall must lead so that the sheet-hand can give the job the maximum grunt potential.

If the staysail is set on a boom, different concepts apply. These will be discussed later in the book, as well as the running gear for jib topsails, topsails, and various other more exotic rags of canvas.

MAKING FAST

One thing a traditional sailor generally does better than his counterpart on a modern Bermudan vessel is handle ropes. Today's yachtsman normally has a winch between him and the action. So long as there are three turns or more on the barrel, the insulation is complete. The only time he may require the skills to deal with loaded ropes is in tying up the yacht. Bad habits can be expensive then, but they rarely are at today's standard floating pontoons.

The gaff sailor, on the other hand, is dealing directly with halyards which may be loaded to half a ton or more. If someone takes the turns off the peak halyard belay before the correct moment, he will be awarded a serious rope burn, or be propelled into orbit. The main halyards must be belayed securely, but in such a way that they cannot lock up, otherwise nothing will clear them short of some smart work with the handy billy, which could be far from convenient.

The answer is simple. Lead a rope to a cleat or pin so that its first half-turn goes straight on, and not so that the second can jam it up. Then start putting on figures of eight. Two or three will usually be enough. When the rope is fast, you must decide upon whether or not to use a locking hitch, or back-turn.

Belaying to a pin

Similar rules apply to a cleat. The important thing is that the rope's initial turns are made so that it can't jam under load.

Good   Good   Bad - this rope can jam on the pin

In the past, there was no decision to be made: you didn't. Ever. Because if the natural fibre rope became wet it would shrink and could lock up inextricably. This will not happen with today's cordage, so you may feel that if there is any danger of a rope being kicked, nudged, or washed off its pin, it would be more secure with a locking hitch. If so, do it, but be aware of the dangers, and never, never, put on a locking hitch before at least two full figures of eight are on the pin underneath it.

The same philosophy applies to mooring lines.

On very large craft, halyards are arranged so that a number of hands can heave at them together. This is often facilitated by a single turning block near deck level. The block is generally either a snatch block or an open sheave. One or two crew swing down on the fall, with the rest tailing on along the deck, 'south' of the turning block. If the loads are heavy, the only way to transfer the halyard to the pin in order to belay, is to clap a stopper* onto the bight. The mate will do this while all hands hang on to their gains. Once the stopper is on, the halyard can be removed from the turning block and made fast.

If the weight is less of a problem, the transfer can be made by the crewman nearest the pin, who will also be the first of those swinging down. On the command, 'slack up', he whips the bight onto the pin. This requires great skill and sureness of hand. It is also highly dangerous, because if he misses his turn he will be launched aloft at rocket-ship speed, having smashed his fingers on the belaying pin as he went by.

COILING

All three-strand ropes are made to be coiled right-handed, or 'clockwise', or 'with the sun' (as seen in the northern hemisphere). They should be coiled naturally, never forced around an elbow or submitted to any other form of brutalisation. They can be coiled on deck if they are too big to handle, otherwise they are best coiled into the left hand with the right doing the work.

Happiness is a well coiled rope.

Swigging the topsail halyard is necessary, even when it's calm. Note staysail sheet pendants and bulls eyes

Always start with the end made fast, so that the kinks can be thrown off the loose end. If you coil the other way, you'll end up with a mess, just as you will with an anti-clockwise coil. You can escape the rewards of these atrocities on a small Bermudan sloop, but even a 25ft gaffer has a peak halyard far longer than the longest rope on a 'three-cornered' 40-footer. Mess rope around, and you're in for trouble. Treat it sweetly, and it will serve for years.

HAULING

The technique of pulling a rope horizontally in a standing position is very simple, but requires confidence. Don't lean forward to get a grip, then bow over the rope and try to pull. Take hold of it right where you are, then move your feet forward and lean steadily so that your thigh and back muscles do the work. You'll be four times as effective, and you won't look like the sainted fish out of water.

If you find yourself pulling in concert with two or three mates, make sure you are all in the 'tug of war' position described above, then concentrate your joint efforts in combined deep jerks. Someone should sing out a rhythm for this, and not be embarrassed, because otherwise you'll never get it together. It needn't be a salty chanty. '1-2-3-heave' does the trick, but for some inexplicable reason, '2-6-hevee!' is far better.

Swigging

Swigging a rope on a cleat to gain that last foot or two of advantage is hard to describe, but vital to master. As in the straight pull, confidence is all.

The method employed is slightly different depending upon whether one or two people are available. If there are two of you, one takes half a figure of eight on the pin or cleat and leans back hard on the tail. The other grabs hold of the bight round about eye-level (NOT way above the head) and throws his weight back with arms extended. The gaff, or the jib, or whatever the load is, will move upward a foot or so. Now, the active party bends his arms while weighing down on the rope, and moves the bight back into line, bearing down the whole time. During this last part of the operation his mate takes up the slack around the pin then holds on while the swigger helps himself to a fresh grip.

Half a figure of eight around the pin often produces more friction than is wanted or needed. If so, use a half turn around the bottom. If you opt for this, the person holding the turn needs to hang on hard, otherwise the poor sailor leaning back will end up flat on the deck. It's amazing how much power an active pair can generate using this method. It works for sheets as well as halyards, and is one of the basic 'motor skills' of the traditional seaman. If the load is lighter, the job can be done singlehanded. A right-handed person will swig back on the strong hand while holding the half-turn fast with the left. A further refinement for the singlehander is to leave the rope belayed with the absolute minimum of turns on the cleat, swig the bight two-handed, then bear down the slack with one hand while taking it up on the cleat with the other.

CHAPTER VI

MAINSAILS

MAINSAIL CUT

Within the basic definition, gaff mainsails vary considerably in shape. Except in unusual cases, however, there are only two cuts. Traditional working sails were cut vertically, primarily for reasons of strength. A sail invariably fails at a seam, if it is to fail at all, and the natural tendency of any mainsail is to split from luff to leech. If this happens anywhere below the deepest set of reef points, the day can still be saved, because the sail can be reefed as a temporary expedient to contain the damage. If the damage occurs above the last reef, you are in big trouble, especially if your sail is cross-cut with seams running with the tear. Such catastrophic disintegration of a vertically cut sail is virtually impossible.

Another benefit of the vertical cut is that reef points can be attached on the seams, no further reinforcement being required. This is not the case with a cross-cut sail.

When gaff was in its prime as a yachting rig, most boats with any pretensions to performance chose cross-cutting. It was felt that since the air was blowing across the sail, the seams would cause less wind resistance. Scientific investigations have shown that with modern sail cloths this is no longer the case, if indeed it ever was. The other advantage of cross-cutting still remains. It is easier for a sailmaker to cut the flow into a cross-cut sail, and judging by the shape of the mainsails in early photographs of racing yachts, sailmakers had perfected this art. The camber* sweeps aft in a sweet, gentle curve, and there is not a trace of that devastating hook in the leech which wrecks the performance of so many gaff sails.

BOOM ANGLE

The angle the boom makes with the deck is an interesting feature of many gaffers, particularly cutters with their long-footed mainsails, and those schooners which boast a serious main boom. Once again, there is a difference between vessels rigged for operating in rough, open water, and those yachts whose prime function was to be 'darlings of the summer day'. Craft used in sheltered water carry their boom ends low,

A loose-footed, vertical cut working gaff mainsail

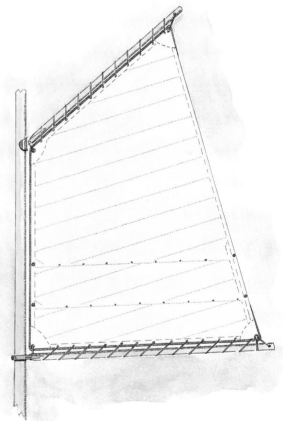

A cross-cut "yacht" mainsail

sometimes nearly parallel to the deck, in order to get the most from their potential sail area. The sea-boat keeps her boom well up.

I wondered about this for years. The reason may seem obvious now, but for me it was bitter experience that supplied the answer. All my boats (working craft every one, except for a yacht built on fishing vessel lines in 1897) had their mainsails cut like yachts, and every time they began tramping on a broad reach in a big sea, they sent me grey with worry by dipping the ends of their long booms into the rushing water. The only answer to the destructive snatching was to rig a boom preventer (see Chapter XIII), but the force imposed on the goose necks was awful. In extreme instances I'd top up the boom with the weather lift as we sailed along. This helped, but caused the gaff and topsail to drift destructively away to leeward.

Pictures of Bristol Channel Pilot Cutters suggested that booms were always carried at a positively jaunty angle. It looked good, and I fondly imagined that the reason was pure fashion. Then, just before I ordered a new mainsail for my own pilot cutter, the revelation came. The mainsails were cut that way so that when they were squared off the boom would stay out of the water on the leeward roll. I had my new sail cut accordingly, and received the reward of fifteen years' grief. It now only dips in the most extreme circumstances.

BENDING ON A MAINSAIL

Bending on a big gaff main short-handed can be a daunting proposition, but if the job is handled systematically it is easy. The same method works well on a smaller sail.

1 — Unfold the sail, and lay it out along the deck as near to the boom as is practical. The boom should be at its normal resting height, supported either by its topping lifts or its gallows if there are any. Take care to arrange the throat, peak, tack and clew in the right area of the boom.

2 — Secure the throat of the sail to the gaff. This is often achieved with a shackle, but a carefully executed lashing will do, particularly if the line is of man-made fibre.

3 — Haul the peak up to its place on the gaff. On large craft this is sometimes done by means of a single block lashed to the gaff end. There is also a hole bored awthwartships through the gaff to assist the outhauling process. The peak lashing is started at the cringle, or earing, of the sail, then taken through the block or the hole. When it has been passed again through the cringle, you have made up a simple but effective purchase. Using this, the head of the sail can be stretched tight. A length of outhaul will be left over, which can be passed through the same route as before to firm things up and add extra security. The peak lashing is finished with a couple of turns through the cringle and around the gaff itself before being hitched off.

4 — Now that the head of the sail is stretched, that part of the job is completed with either a lacing or a series of individual lashings called robands. If you opt for a lacing, it is best taken round the boom and the lacing eyes in one uninterrupted spiral.

The benefits of a lacing are two-fold, though you may feel that these are not enough. It is easy and quick to rig, and it is self-adjusting, so that each lacing eye takes an equal portion of the load. Unfortunately, a lacing suffers from a grave disadvantage: it is exceedingly prone to chafe, and if it should break, it will unravel in no time. To rig it with a series of marline hitches rather than a round lacing would not stop the chafe, though it would give you a little longer to sort things out by being slower to unravel after one part has let go.

Use robands instead. The term roband probably has developed as a diminutive of 'rope bands', and this is precisely what they are. Each lacing eye has its own lashing to the gaff. The individual roband is a length of line, long enough to pass twice round the gaff, through the lacing eye, and be finished off with a reef-knot, whose ends are either seized, or passed back through the lay of the lacing. The latter is quicker and more secure. Robands take more effort but are far better in the long run. Gaff lacings always choose to let go miles from land, in a rising gale, just as night is approaching.

5 — Now hoist the sail steadily with throat and peak, so as to keep the gaff parallel with the boom. As the sail goes up, either pass the luff lacing, or seize or shackle the luff eyelets to the mast hoops. When the last eyelet has been attended to, secure the tack to either the goose neck or the forward end of the boom with a shackle or a lashing.

If the sail is loose-footed, the tack may be carried on a downhaul rather than being permanently attached. This gives it the potential for being triced aloft by a light line rigged through a turning block at the gaff jaws. If your boat is kitted out like this, she will almost certainly have mast hoops as well to control the luff when the tack is triced. The system is a tremendous boon when manoeuvring under sail (see Chapter XV).

The main advantage of a luff lacing over mast hoops is that in the long-term it will do less damage to the shaft of the mast and cause less annoyance in the event of a few hoops being broken. Sliding a new hoop over the masthead is not a practicable proposition because of all the standing and running rigging. For this reason, it is worth installing at least one spare when fitting out. It can then idle below the working ones until its moment of glory comes, as come it will on a long cruise.

6 — If there is a wind blowing, you'll be growing tired of fighting the half-controlled sail by now, so before bending on the clew and really powering things up, lower the peak until the breeze looses interest.

7 — If the mainsail is over 350sq ft, you'll probably need power of some sort to stretch out the clew. Should the sail be set loose-footed on the boom, this will be supplied by the main clew outhaul. The clew of a loose-footed sail is never left supported entirely on its outhaul because if it should part when the topping lifts are overhauled, the sail will go wild and the boom will massacre the watch on deck. Sometimes a leathered traveller, similar to a bowsprit traveller is used to take the weight. Other boats prefer a short horse running fore and aft on the boom to which the clew is shackled. Even a stout lashing will serve.

If the sail is laced to the boom, the outhaul will be a lesser creature. You may therefore need to rig up a small tackle temporarily to the boom end. The question of how much tension to put on a laced foot before permanently attaching the clew to the

A first-class arrangement for the clew of a loose-footed mainsail aboard Freya.

boom can only be found by trial and error. It will depend upon how the sail has been cut, perhaps upon the weather as well. If in doubt, err on the tight side, unless the sail is of natural fibre. In this case it will require delicate handling through the stretching-in period (Appendix 1). Your sailmaker can advise you best about that. Once the sail is settled in, however, remember that if you set the outhaul up tightly when the weather is warm and dry, the canvas will try to shrink when it subsequently gets wet. Unless you can accommodate its wishes, it will resent the treatment it is receiving.

A foot lacing is best rove like a gaff lacing — round and round — so that the pull evens up. It is less prone to chafe than its brother aloft, and even if it does come adrift, rigging a new one or knotting it up temporarily is an undramatic affair.

8 — The tensioning of a loose-footed sail is one of the joys of an unlaced foot. The outhaul can be eased off in light airs to increase the curvature and hence the power of the sail. The canvas can also be hauled flat in a harder breeze, particularly while sailing to windward. This will reduce the tendency of the sail to heel the boat and generate weather helm, without a significant drop in power output.

9 — When the four corners of the sail are on, and the lacings and hoops made good, all that remains is to reeve up the reefing pendants. Because of the inconvenience of doing the job at sea, it is worth keeping at least the first two permanently rove. On a long passage it is as well to reeve them all up, because you never know for sure when and how badly conditions will deteriorate. If you need the deep reef halfway through the middle watch, you'll regret not having had the pendant ready beforehand. That is a promise.

Homeward bound.

HOISTING THE SAIL

Ideally, a boat should be head-to-wind to hoist the main, but the important thing is that the breeze is somewhere forward of the beam. Theoretically, one of the benefits of gaff sails as opposed to Bermudan is that they can be hoisted and lowered on any point of sailing, but in a hard breeze this may not be so. Like any canvas set between a mast and a boom, a gaff sail is better behaved if it can spill wind. Here is the ideal sequence of events:

1 — If it is not convenient to come right into the wind, be ready to ease the sheet so that the sail can luff as it goes up.

2 — Overhaul* the mainsheet. Where the boom is resting on gallows, top it up. In the absence of gallows, the topping lifts can be left alone, unless the boom is carried lower at rest than with the sail set.

3 — Cast off the sail ties. If there is a helmsman steering the boat, you might want to leave one made up above his head until the last minute.

4 — Make sure the topsail sheet and ensign halyard are clear to run.

5 — Hoist throat and peak together so that the gaff goes aloft horizontally. Make sure that the gaff is either between the topping lifts, or on the correct side of it if there is only one.

Generally, the halyards are arranged in such a way that the peak naturally rises faster than the throat. If this is allowed to happen, the poor soul pulling the throat will soon be on his knees, because the weight of the gaff will be transferred to his department by the famous force of gravity.

Hoisting the mainsail

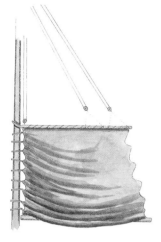

⇐
Note that the gaff is kept parallel to the boom in order to ease the strain on the throat halyard.

⇒
Once the throat is well stretched, peak the sail up until wrinkles appear between peak and tack. These will disappear when the sail draws.

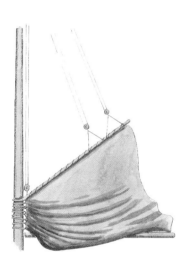

Lowering the mainsail
The gaff is kept peaked up as the sail is lowered, so that its weight pushes down on the throat.

6 — When the throat is almost up, belay the peak and swig up the throat. Finish it off with its purchase if necessary. After you are satisfied that the luff is tight enough, turn your attention to the peak.

7 — Heave the peak up until you see distinct wrinkles develop between the peak of the sail and the tack. If you don't see these, you haven't peaked up enough, regardless of the material of the sail. They should still be visible even after the topping lift is eased, but they will disappear when the sail fills with wind. If the air is light and they don't quite vanish, ease the peak an inch or two until they do.

8 — Ease away the topping lift. At no time should the lift be allowed to 'girt' across the lee side of the sail, causing chafe and ruining the set.

9 — Coil down and go sailing.

DROPPING THE SAIL

Dropping the main is more or less a reverse of the hoisting process, but there are a few points to note. Once again, try to let the sail spill wind. It makes all the difference. If you cannot manage to bring the boat head-to-wind, drop the sail with sheet eased, but be ready to haul the boom inboard as soon as the sail is well on the way down, to keep the canvas out of the water.

1 — Make sure both halyards are clear to run. Where there is any chance of losing the ends aloft, make them fast now.

2 — Rig sail-ties ready over the boom.

3 — Top up the boom, if necessary, to its resting height, or just above the level of the gallows. If the boom's sailing angle is higher than its resting angle, just take up the slack in the topping lifts.

4 — Don't forget the chimney. When the stove is hot, arrange your manoeuvre to bring the sail down on the other side deck. If you drop it onto the 'Charlie Noble', you'll have a hole to mend. I've done it twice...

5 — Overhaul any halyard purchases, then lower away with both halyards together, but keep the peak above the throat at all times. If you don't, the laws of geometry will see to it that the sail refuses to come down.

6 — On a boat with a boom too heavy to man-handle, a hand should be detailed off to make the mainsheet up hard as soon as the sail is down. If the sheet is left loose, the boom will swing around while the crew are trying to stow the sail, throwing them off like rats from a terrier.

7 — If your engine is turning, make sure that neither the topsail sheet nor the ensign halyard have even half a chance of getting themselves into the propeller.

8 — When the sail is down, leave the gaff parallel to the boom for stowing, with a small gap between the two spars.

STOWING

There are a number of ways of doing this. They are all correct, so long as they result in a neat, tight stow. Here is one that works on small sails, and is fine at least as far up as 800sq ft.

1 — If the boom's normal resting height is such that there is going to be a struggle, lower it with the topping lifts until you can reach the sail easily, taking up slack on the sheet as you go. You'll have to ease the peak halyards as well, in order to keep the gaff in touch with the boom. On a big boat, this extra trouble is often worthwhile. Once the sail is stowed neatly, you can top up the whole boom/gaff assembly to its proper attitude.

2 — The mate takes the leech of the sail and starting at the peak, works down to the clew, hauling aft all the way, assisted by more of the crew if necessary. This removes any bunch-ups of canvas.

3 — Starting 2ft or 3ft above the clew, he then proceeds up the leech, bundling the sail into the 'bag' he has made, while all hands follow suit along the bunt, or body of the sail.

4 — With the sail loosely packaged, the crew now work together to shake it into a

*Sail handling aboard
a well run smack.*

neater stow, before rolling it tightly up onto the boom, to secure it with the ties. These are led over the gaff and under the foot of the sail, but not around the boom. Sometimes, ties are seen led below the gaff, directly round the head of the sail. It is tempting to do this if the crew are experiencing difficulty reaching the gaff, but the practice should be avoided like a rotten oyster. It looks exceedingly unsightly, and causes unnecessary stretch in the head-rope of the sail.

5 — The best gaff sail-ties are of heavy webbing with a loop stitched into one end. If these are not available, you can manage fine with lengths of stout rope, whipped at one end with an eye spliced into the other. By passing the whipped end through the eye after it has gone round the sail, a modest purchase can be achieved for sweating up a tight stow, and the tie can be readily made off with a slippery half-hitch.

6 — If the sail is loose-footed, ignore the instruction about shaking the roll, or else the stow will fall out from under the foot, and you'll have to start again.

7 — At some stage, depending on the way the sail has fallen, you'll have to tidy up the topsail sheet and ensign halyard.

8 — When the stow is complete, the gaff angle can be set to suit your taste. Personally I like to see it parallel, or slightly up at the throat, but that is only my own opinion. Scandinavians keep their peaks well up, indicating that beauty, in this matter at least, is definitely in the eye of the beholder.

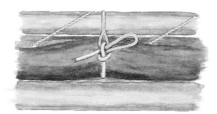

*Tying up the sail
with a slippery hitch*

*Note that the sail tie
passes over the gaff
- between the foot of
the sail and the boom.*

CHAPTER VII

TOPSAILS

Topsails are the glory and the curse of gaff rig. A good topsail is worth at least a knot on any point of sailing to a 32ft cutter in force 3, while the value of a full set of topsails plus a fisherman staysail to a schooner is so great that taking them in with the wind below force 5 is like throwing a sea anchor over the stern.

Working with topsails is an art. There are so many variables that the chances of getting it right first time on a strange boat are as good as nil. Yet those very uncertainties make the sail so flexible that if the effort is made, it must set well in the end.

A badly setting topsail makes a vessel heel excessively and does nothing for her forward movement. If it is working properly, the sail is worth every penny you paid for it. It stands high up where the wind is blowing more strongly. It has only a thin topmast or topsail yard* between it and the clean air which it is cutting. Thus, it suffers far less than the mainsail from interference due to the woodwork. So long as it can be sheeted to maintain its maximum curvature in its forward part, it is delivering the goods. There are only two catches: you must get it up there and coax it to perform. Then you have to persuade it to come down again.

Despite numerous differences in detail, all topsails have their essential running rigging and nomenclature in common. The halyard hoists the sail, or the yard and the sail. The downhaul tensions the luff and supplies the force to make any yard stand correctly. The sheet is bent onto clew or jackyard* and outhauls the sail to the gaff end.

Topsails fall into two main families: those which are kept permanently bent on aloft, and those which are sent up from the deck.

HOOPED TOPSAILS

The permanently rigged sail is the easiest to set, but because it needs a hand aloft to put a tidy stow on it, or to cast off the gaskets*, it is usually reserved for craft of over 50ft. This type always uses a topmast, and the upper part of the luff is attached to it by hoops, just like a mainsail. The sail may have a short yard, or 'headstick' at the upper end of its luff. The lower part of the luff is often cut away to clear the lower masthead, while the tack is secured to a downhaul set up from the deck. The sheet passes outboard to the end of the gaff, thence to the gaff jaws, and so to the deck for trimming.

All that is needed to hoist this sail is to cast off the gaskets, heave away on the halyard until it is mastheaded, set up the downhaul, then sheet in. This can generally be done on any point of sailing, though the cleanest results are achieved when close-hauled with the sail to leeward. Dropping the sail should present as few problems.

Some topsails of this type are rigged with a simple brail so that they can be doused from the deck. This makes life easier and safer for the hand aloft, and is a system adopted by many schooners. On many such craft, brailing alone keeps the sail quiet in moderate conditions, which saves the trouble of sending anyone up to secure the gaskets.

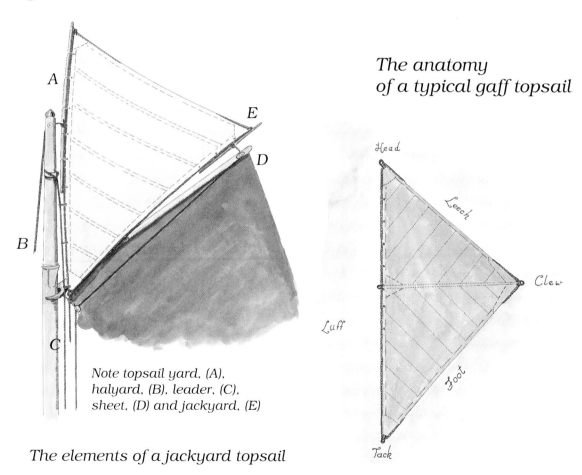

*Note topsail yard, (A),
halyard, (B), leader, (C),
sheet, (D) and jackyard, (E)*

The elements of a jackyard topsail

*The anatomy
of a typical gaff topsail*

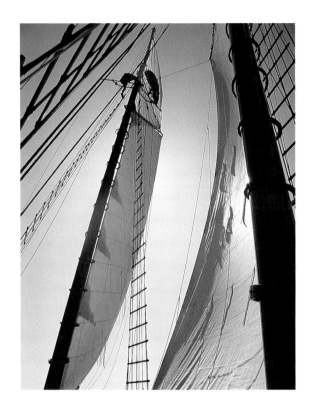

A topsail set from hoops stands well, but requires tending from aloft.

TOPSAILS SET FLYING

A small topsail, whether or not it has a yard, can sometimes be set flying with no more gear than its halyard, downhaul and sheet. There will be a tendency, however, for the luff to sag out from the mast as the breeze hardens. This becomes more pronounced on topsails over about 100sq ft, and is usually counteracted by rigging a leader.

A leader is a length of line spliced round the topmast (or upper mast on a 'pole'), and brought loosely down to the deck on the same side as the rest of the topsail gear. The topsail luff has one or more hanks on it which are attached to this. When the sail is hoisted and the tack has been bowsed down, the leader is hardened up, pulling the luff in to the mast. Once this has been done, and not before, the sheet can be hauled tight.

Some larger vessels carry two leaders, one for the lower part of the luff below the main mast cap, the other for the topmast. It helps to have a tackle to set up the leader, but one ingenious method is to rig it through a turning block at the deck, then shackle its end to the lower block of the topsail tack downhaul. This has the merit of two tackles for the price of one. As you pull down on the tack, you are also tensioning the leader. It works a treat.

Hoisting a yard topsail is an easy two person job on a quiet day — even on a big one.

HOISTING A TOPSAIL

Here is a systematic process for setting a simple, jib-headed topsail*. Such a sail is hoisted most easily either head-to-wind, or sailing close-hauled. If you are under way and the sail is to leeward of the mainsail it will go up without interruption, but you will be working on the 'downhill' side of the boat. Furthermore, the belly of the mainsail often makes it impossible to see what is going on aloft. If the topsail is on the windward side, it must be persuaded to force a passage across the gaff, the topping lift (if the sail is outside it), and all the peak halyards. Neither is ideal, but it has been observed that in this life, little is.

The further off the wind you steer, the more awkward things become on the lee side, until finally it is impossible to squeeze the sail between the bunt of the mainsail, the gaff, and the shrouds. On the weather side, matters remain more or less the same for the jib-header, except that once the breeze is well abaft the beam it is inconvenient to 'luff' the sail away from the peak halyards by steering above the set of the sails during the hoist, which is always a possibility when close reaching.

Let's assume then, that you are close-hauled on the port tack and you want to hoist your jib-headed topsail:

1 — Sheet, halyard and downhaul should be permanently stowed near the mast on the port side. All these are attached to the sail by the means provided — usually shackles — after first checking aloft to ensure that they are cleared away. There is no particular order; just be certain that the sail has no kinks in it. This is best ascertained by running the luff through your hands in between shackling on the halyard and the tack downhaul.

2 — When all three are secure, hank the luff of the sail to the leader, which should be sagging away from the mast to simplify the job. Some craft used to employ a permanently tight jackstay instead of a leader, but these are rarely seen today.

3 — Hoist the sail, taking the weight on the halyard and sheet together. This achieves two things: the modest load on the sheet will dissuade it from performing its party piece and taking a turn round the end of the gaff. If it ever succeeds in this, it's checkmate. You've either to walk the gaff, or lower the main to sort out the mess. The sheet never clears itself. The other advantage of using the sheet to help hoist is that you stop the sail rucking up against the 'cat's cradle' of the peak halyards. You can let it do this ten times and all will be well. On the eleventh, right in front of the yacht club balcony, the canvas will jam itself under a span, or be sucked into a hook, or some such horror.

4 — When the sail is almost up, make fast the sheet, but don't pull it right home.

5 — Now masthead the halyard, and don't be satisfied until you've stretched it to within an ace of discovering its breaking strain. You must do this because you are about to seriously power up the downhaul. If you haven't stretched the halyard, the downhaul purchase will do it for you and you'll end up with an unsheetable topsail, funereally hoisted to a half-mast position.

6 — When you're satisfied with the halyard, crank on the downhaul as hard as seems reasonable on the day. Don't pull the tack out of the sail if there's only 5 knots of breeze, but if there is a smart blow, give it a serious tug.

7 — Now you can heave up the leader. That won't take a second.

8 — Lastly, sheet in the sail. If there's a useful breeze, try to set it as flat as you can. It's impossible to oversheet the majority of topsails in a working wind, but if the wind falls light, try easing the sheet to put some more draught into the sail.

Topsail setting

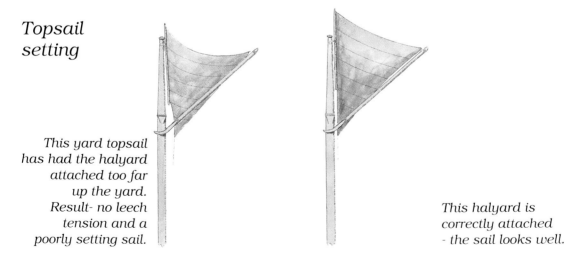

This yard topsail has had the halyard attached too far up the yard. Result- no leech tension and a poorly setting sail.

This halyard is correctly attached - the sail looks well.

The hoisting procedure is the same if the topsail has a yard, except that you now have a choice of where to attach the halyard. There are numerous ways of bending it on, but the chosen method should permit you to move it to different positions on the yard. The topsail sheet, like any other, needs to lead correctly. This can be significantly altered by moving the halyard a foot down the yard. Where there is a jackyard involved, the same applies.

In a perfect rig, the topsail yard will balance at the correct attachment point for its halyard. It may even under-balance a touch, so that its tendency is to swivel 'right way up'. Sadly, in our less than ideal world, it more often than not ends up over-balancing in an attempt to secure the height necessary for the correct sheeting angle. This makes life somewhat more interesting for the crew, but otherwise it is nothing to worry about.

When a yard topsail is being hoisted, the downhaul should be manned as well as the halyard and sheet, if there are sufficient bodies available. If not, forget the sheet and hope for the best, or try to keep the sail to leeward, which at least removes the menace of the peak halyard trap. Any leader will be rigged on the lower part of the luff, with the yard extending the upper section above the masthead.

A serious jackyard topsail.

As the yard goes aloft, maintain some pressure from the downhaul to keep it horizontal, or pointing slightly upwards. A vertical yard will act like a javelin if it is to windward, spearing every likely aperture, and favouring the peak halyard as a matter of course. When its upper end is clear of danger, you can begin bringing it upright, but don't exert any real downhaul tension until you have stretched the halyard tight. Now set up the downhaul as for a jib-header, and the yard should cock up like the cantilever that it is. Harden up the leader, sheet home, and coil down.

In theory, yard topsails should be more easily hoisted to leeward. Usually they aren't, because of the awkwardness of being downhill and unsighted. There is also the psychological factor: the wind is always blowing harder in the slot twixt main and staysail, which is exactly where you are standing for a leeward topsail hoist. The effect on morale is dismal. I usually end up chickening out of the project, only to regret it ten minutes later when I toddle up forward with the lads to give it another try.

Topsail sheets are a notoriously heavy pull. Some crews get round the problem by over-peaking the gaff before hoisting the topsail. After they've done their best with the sheet, they 'settle' the peak until the topsail is drawing to their satisfaction. I see nothing wrong with this, so long as the greatest of care is exercised at the settling stage. Anyone who lets the last turn off the peak purchase should have his grog stopped, and if he lets the halyard run, he should be sent the sailmaker's bill.

LOWERING A TOPSAIL

The essentials of lowering a topsail are simple: first make sure the sheet and halyard are clear to run. Ease and release the sheet, then let off the halyard. This is removed from the pin on all but the largest vessels, but it is kept in hand while the sail is brought in by the downhaul. Whatever you do, never allow the topsail halyard any chance of escaping up the mast. It goes through the highest sheave on the boat, and if you can't lower your topmast easily, the only way of re-reeving will be to shin up the bare pole.

With the wind forward of the beam, any topsail will always be willing to oblige on the leeward side, so long as you don't mind getting your feet wet and having a fight to keep it on board. Topsails with heavy yards can be tiresome in this respect. Unfortunately, yards, particularly jackyards, are inclined sometimes to play games when invited to come down on the windward side in a hard breeze. So long as they can be persuaded to remain horizontal or slightly cocked up, all should be well, and once the sail is being blown against the weather side of the main, the job is easy, whatever the conditions. If the mainsail has a laced foot, the topsail yard will sometimes lie quietly on top of the main boom, while you gather your wits and de-rig the sail.

Even when running, you are still in with a fair chance of dragging down your topsail to windward. To leeward, you would have no hope at all.

Taken by and large, if you can deal with your topsail on the weather side, you'll probably have less trouble with it. In extremis, it will always capitulate if you can arrange to be close-hauled on the right tack to set it to leeward.

THE FISHERMAN STAYSAIL

This glorious square of canvas is found only on schooners. Its name is a reference to the great Grand Bankers of North America, amongst whom the sail was a speciality. It is four-cornered, with all of them set flying. There are two halyards, one to each mast, a tack downhaul which tensions the luff abaft the foremast, and a sheet which is normally led through a block near the end of the main boom.

Hoisting a fisherman is entirely logical. Like any other type of topsail, the sheet is the last rope to be pulled, because the sail is extremely powerful and very lively indeed. As soon as it has wind in it, the halyard men might as well jump over the side if their task is not completed.

On a long reach, the sail is set to windward of the foresail gaff, but to leeward of the triatic stays. If you work hard enough, you might persuade the fore topsail to set behind it at certain clearly defined angles to the wind, which can only be determined by experiment.

Close-hauled, a fisherman staysail must be hoisted to leeward, which means that the sail is fully lowered at every tack or gybe. Schooners involved in serious inshore racing carry two 'fishermen' and run them up and down at every new board. Both throat and peak halyards are double-ended, so that either side can be the hauling side. Nobody gets bored on a schooner.

On a windy day it makes a lot of sense to hoist the fisherman 'in stops'. This means that the sail is prepared with all four corners cleared and no twists in the bunt, then the main part of the sail is flaked carefully into a tight roll. This is stopped up with rotten caulking cotton or, more usually nowadays, cheap rubber bands.

The roll is sent aloft, and the halyards mastheaded. At the word, tack and sheet are pulled, the stops break out, the sail fills with a bang to wake the dead and the schooner heels until her waterways run green. Then she changes gear, and the power is something everyone should feel just once in their lives. If she's racing, the opposition can only watch her as she sails them hull-down in a short afternoon.

The fisherman staysail set on a reach

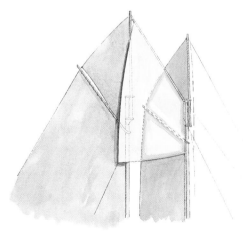

This depiction is of the lee side of the rig. The luff of the sail is to windward of the foresail and fore topsail, so that these can be eased away without interfering with the set of the fisherman. Note the leech of the sail to leeward of the main and main topsail. The whole sail will be setting to leeward of the triatic stay and the topmast stays.

71

CHAPTER VIII

HEADSAILS

It is almost unheard of for a yacht or small fore-and-aft rigged working craft to offer her crew a choice of mainsails. Most, however, carry a selection of headsails to suit different conditions. In later chapters we'll be looking at the variety of large jibs, staysails and spinnakers with which a boat can propel herself in light or moderate going. The purpose of this section is to come to grips with working sails only.

Whether or not any jibs are carried, the staysail can truthfully be called the power-house of a gaff-rigged vessel. Unless the boat is cat-rigged with an undivided sail area, the mainsail alone is not generally very effective, especially when the wind is forward of the beam. She is unbalanced and the main's drive is in an unenhanced state.

In order to answer their helms in a satisfactory manner all sailing craft require some sail area forward of their centre of lateral resistance and some abaft it. In a sloop, the mainsail itself supplies some of the forward part of this balance, in a cutter it gives very little. Thus, a sloop will usually sail after a fashion without a staysail. A cutter will have no great interest in going anywhere before some canvas has been hoisted forward of the mast. The situation in a schooner or ketch is of course more complex. Nonetheless, neither of these craft perform at all well until a headsail is up and drawing.

If the boat has a cutter foretriangle she may balance reasonably under a jib hoisted without a staysail; she will, however, lack power. The slot between the jib and the main is far too wide to squeeze the air passing through into the Venturi effect which generates so much drive. Hoist the staysail, and you have two Venturis working at once.

On a cutter, a staysail with no jib will still slot the air sweetly around the back of the mainsail, but the boat will carry more weather helm than she wants until a jib is deployed. With the jib up, the boat should positively leap into life.

The business of hoisting and lowering a staysail rarely causes any problem, even on a sloop, whose crew may have to venture onto the bowsprit. This is because the staysail, by definition, is hanked onto the forestay, and is therefore always under control. The only part of it which can 'escape' is the clew, and if this should run amok through losing its sheets you have only to lower the sail down the stay to restore peace and tranquillity.

In the old days, hanks were 'standing' items. They were threaded onto the forestay before it was connected at its lower end or passed through the stem. The eyelets in the luff of the sail were seized permanently to the hanks, and the tack was shackled to the stemhead. The only readily removable item was the halyard. Now, almost all staysails are fitted with piston hanks, which offer the inestimable advantage of allowing the sail to be unbent quickly and stowed in a bag out of the sun and the rain. The traditional system worked adequately with flax sails that were in daily use. Polyester cloth which spends much of its year idle has different priorities if it is to give long service (see Chapter XVI).

All you have to do to bend on the sail is shackle or hook on the tack, hank on the luff, running it through your hands as you do to make sure it has no twists, then attach the sheets. I prefer to use bowlines for this, though some folks like to shackle them on. It's not so important with staysails, but when talking about jibs I will enlarge on this preference (see page 76). If you like to hook on the halyard before you are ready to hoist the sail, be sure to put a 'head-stop' around the top hank to hold the sail down. Boats that don't do this always look unseamanlike, with the halyard hanging in a bight under the forestay because it is impossible to pull up the slack without taking the sail with it.

Like any working headsail, the staysail can be hoisted and dropped on any point of sailing. It will go up more readily if the sheets are kept eased until the halyard is belayed, but lowering the sail is often less dramatic if the sheet is left made up until the canvas is safely down on deck.

A loose-footed staysail can be prettily stowed by taking off the halyard, leaving the sail hanked on, rolling the canvas neatly, stopping it up, and hooking the halyard onto the clew. The clew is then hoisted above head height, and the sail is kept from swinging around by tensioning the sheets. The sail is now ready for use, but the foredeck is kept clear — a particular benefit when dirty work with the ground tackle is anticipated.

Boomed staysails

Many gaffers carry their staysails on a full-length boom, or a short one near the clew known as a club*. The sail may be fully or partially laced to the spar if it is pivoted at the forestay. Some booms, however, are pivoted from a fitting sited abaft the stem. A sail will not be laced to such a boom, and it scores highly in terms of power because as the sheet is eased, the sail becomes fuller by a trick of geometry.

The great bonus afforded by the boomed staysail is that once the sheet is set up for close-hauled sailing it requires no further attention. When you tack, you can forget all about it. It will flop over of its own accord, which is useful if you have running backstays to handle. Another positive feature is that the boom can sometimes be persuaded to hold the staysail clear out to windward on a run, with the application of a minimum of extra knitting.

On the negative side, many booms are sheeted to horses across the foredeck. These trip you up on dark nights. They also keep the whole ship awake as the helmsman allows the staysail to fall into the mainsail's wind shadow on a broad reach, so that the shackle clatters across with a deathly crash. Furthermore, there is the question of the staysail boom knocking people overboard in similar circumstances. A boom without a horse will be better behaved, but the sail won't stand so well, because either the clew will be too close to the centreline of the boat on the wind, or, if it is eased, the sail will twist too much, with the upper third refusing duty.

JIBS

Jibs on gaffers are invariably set on the bowsprit. On very large vessels more than one may be carried, in which case they will be hanked to various upper stays, while in smaller craft with clipper bows and the shorter, stoutly rigged bowsprits which go with them, jibs are also hanked-on. Occasionally, such an arrangement is also seen on a spoon-bowed yacht, but the favoured system in most vessels, especially in Europe, is to set the jib 'flying'.

*Hooking on the jib tack
aboard a Norwegian cutter.*

Hanked-on Jibs

Whether it is tacked down on a bowsprit or a long jib-boom*, a hanked-on jib is treated in more or less the same manner as a staysail. It will probably be cut higher in the clew in order to stop it picking up a bunt-full of sea if the ship dips her bowsprit, but that apart, the only real difference is that it may be rigged with a downhaul.

A downhaul is secured to the head of the sail after being led through a turning block near the tack. From there it runs inboard to the foredeck. When the sail is hoisted it carries the downhaul up with it, and this makes it essential to flake the line down clear to run before manning the halyard. If it jams, of course, the sail won't go any further up the stay.

74

When the jib has to come in, you should cast off the halyard and haul away on the downhaul before anyone goes near the bowsprit. Bowsprits are dangerous enough without having to indulge in unnecessary heroics. The downhaul will do most of the bowsprit hand's job, because not only will it kill the sail, it will also act as that vital head-stop. As soon as the downhaul has been made fast, the crew can lay out onto the spar and put the ties onto the sail to keep the sea from licking it off again. Gaskets permanently rigged on the bowsprit rather than a pocketful of sail ties are another life-saver. In short, however stout your foot-ropes, anything which diminishes the time spent out there and which stabilises the situation is worth ten safety harnesses. It's all very well to clip on, and I'm not saying you shouldn't, but being dragged along by a lifeline under the plunging bows of a 30 ton vessel logging 8knots on a dark night is not like an evening out at the Palais. It is infinitely preferable to assume that if you fall, you're dead, then clip on to give yourself a second chance. That way, you'll think seriously about the gear and you'll be far less likely to go for a swim at all.

The Dyarchy Forestay

This system was perfected by the great designer, Jack Giles, for his cruising masterpiece, *Dyarchy*. It incorporates the handling advantages of hanking the jib on with the benefit of being able to do the whole job from inboard.

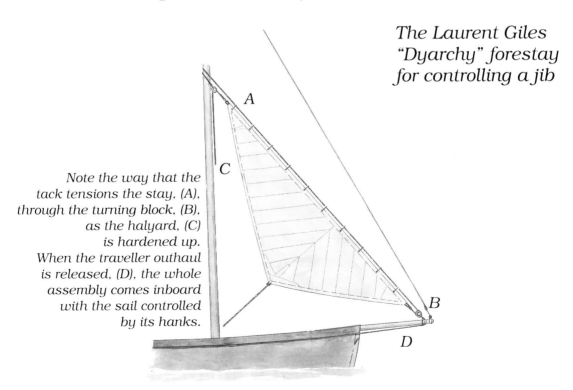

The Laurent Giles "Dyarchy" forestay for controlling a jib

Note the way that the tack tensions the stay, (A), through the turning block, (B), as the halyard, (C) is hardened up. When the traveller outhaul is released, (D), the whole assembly comes inboard with the sail controlled by its hanks.

The jib-stay is of flexible wire. It is dead-ended up the mast in the immediate vicinity of the jib halyard block. From there it leads down through a turning block at the bowsprit end, which may be permanently rigged, or attached to a traveller. The stay is finished off with a hard-eye. The jib tack is shackled to this and the luff is hanked to the standing part which at the moment is under no tension. The halyard is now shackled to the head of the jib. When the sail is hoisted the hanks slide up the jib-stay and as the luff is tensioned the pull from the tack tightens it. The wire then acts as a true secondary forestay, strengthening the mast, and helping the luff of the sail to stand.

As the sail is lowered, it remains under control at all times. When the halyard tension comes off, the standing part of the wire is allowed to sag inboard with the sail still hanked on to it. This makes the job far less fraught with potential horrors than if the sail were set flying (see below). In spite of the genuinely innovative nature of the *Dyarchy* forestay, many owners prefer to set their jibs flying, because of the comparative simplicity, the cheapness, and the authenticity of the older type of gear.

Jibs set flying

The standard gaff rig jib is attached at its three corners only. The head is at the halyard, the sheets, needless to say, are at the clew, and the tack is hooked to a traveller which will carry it out to the bowsprit end. (See photo page 74). Travellers should be oversize — far larger in diameter than the bowsprit. They should also be leathered and kept well greased. So long as these three points have been observed, I've never known one get stuck. The hook is often a tortuous shape known as a pig's tail. This does away with any possibility of the tack worming off when you don't want it to. Unfortunately, it also facilitates achieving a half-turn in the tack which neither the sail nor the skipper will enjoy, should he venture far enough forward of the mast to notice what the crew have done.

The traveller outhaul is rove through a sheave in the bowsprit end, immediately inboard of the cranse iron. It doesn't normally warrant a purchase, though if the jibs are made from flax canvas, a whip may help on vessels over 55ft. In my experience, an inhaul is never necessary. With the wind forward of the beam you have only to cast off the outhaul and the traveller will come in so fast that your biggest concern will be not to lose the end of it. If the wind is aft, so that the sail is 'lifting' the boat along, you may have to give a tug on the sheet to help it inboard, but this is not an energetic business. An inhaul is just something else to snag while you are outhauling the tack of the sail, and what you don't want at any price is for the sail to be hanging around like the Grand Old Duke of York — neither up nor down.

Sheets on the jib should always be attached with a bowline, especially if the sail is set flying. I make no apology for being dogmatic about this because I've tried both ways many times, and shackles have always ended up bringing the crew to tears. I once saw the clew of a brand new sail beaten out of it in seconds by a heavy shackle. The sheet was let go in a storm-force squall, and before things could be brought back in hand, the aft half of the sail had disappeared. Well-tied bowlines in modern rope would not have shaken out. They wouldn't have done any damage either. I've also known a number of people, experienced and otherwise, sustain head injuries from clew shackles in spite of being warned to watch out. In this context, shackles really are dangerous. They also cost money, and in order to rig them you must first take the trouble to splice thimbles into the ends of your sheets, so why on earth bother?

Handling jibs can be fraught with pain if they are given half a chance to run berserk. They are the liveliest sails on board, so careful thought is always needed before hoisting them. The basic system goes like this, although it is sometimes possible to vary it:

    1 — Lay the sail out on the lee side of the foredeck.

    2 — Bring the traveller in to the stemhead and hook on the tack, taking care to avoid twists.

    3 — Follow the foot through, and bend on the lee sheet.

    4 — Take the weather sheet over the forestay and bend it on, ensuring that you have not led it forward of the luff of the jib.

    5 — Shackle or hook on the halyard.

    6 — Haul the tack out to the end of the bowsprit and secure it. Do not allow the sail to drop into the sea if you are under way.

    7 — Hoist away smartly on the halyard until you've got all you can. Make fast.

    8 — If there is a stiff breeze, pull in enough sheet at this stage to settle things down, but don't sheet right home.

    9 — Sweat up the halyard purchase until the luff is really tight.

    10 — Sheet in and coil down.

All this is as easy as pie on the mooring on a calm morning. It's a different story if you're hoisting after changing down jibs on a nasty night. If that's how things are, you might well prefer to do the job hove-to (Chapter X), or on a very broad reach. The former method will ensure that the jib is not dragged into the sea at 7 knots. The latter will give you some lee to work in, behind the mainsail.

In some circumstances it pays to lay out the jib to windward of the forestay instead of to leeward as described above. This is helpful if your boat has no stanchions and guard-rails to keep the sail on board.

Either hoisting or lowering a jib in a breeze is much easier if you have two or three crew on the job. If you are alone on the foredeck, you need to plan carefully before you start exposing canvas to a strong wind.

Dropping the jib

You can argue all night about whether to let go the halyard before the outhaul, or vice versa, but in the end, your decision will depend on the 'state of play' at the time. The one thing you must never do is let the sheet off too soon.

If you are working single-handed and the outhaul is belayed well forward, you might prefer to let go the halyard and drag the sail down by the sheet, then release the outhaul when the sail is safely on deck. This leaves the sail dangling around the bowsprit, so if you're fully crewed you could do better to knock off the outhaul, let the tack whizz inboard, then let go the halyard and have a couple of folks muzzle the sail before it whisks them off the deck.

The answer is to consider carefully what will happen in either case.

As in hoisting, dropping a jib is easy in calm conditions. If it's blowing, you need to take the power out of it somehow, unless you have people you are not fond of lounging around up forward. The easiest way is to run the boat downwind. The mainsail will then divert the breeze out of the jib. As soon as the sail falls limp, let go the outhaul and heave the sail inboard with the sheet, releasing the halyard when it is convenient. This works well, but in a real blow it can be a trifle dangerous if the helmsman isn't concentrating.

The safest technique for dropping the jib in a hard breeze, particularly if the sail has a measure of overlap, is to heave the boat to, so that the jib comes aback with its clew or weather sheet against the forestay.

After the situation has stabilised you can try easing either the outhaul or the halyard and pulling the sail aft by its weather sheet until a sizeable percentage of it is pressed against the windward side of the staysail. It is now effectively neutralised and can be brought in at will. The hove-to equilibrium of the boat will be disturbed by the jib's sudden disappearance, but I haven't yet found a gaffer which will be so shocked she will tack herself in disgust. Don't try anything of the kind if the boat has no forefoot, however. As soon as the jib is gone, she'll spin rudely on her heel and you'll be left like a man sitting on a branch, sawing it off next to the tree-trunk.

Furling gears

Because of the obvious challenges in the handling of jibs, many people have opted over the years to leave them permanently hoisted on a roller furling gear. These admirable items are not to be confused with the heavy-duty roller reefing devices fitted to the forestays of Bermudan vessels. They do not reef sails. They furl them, and that is all. Such equipment has been available for most of the twentieth century. They are reliable, and save a great deal of trauma. They can even be used to facilitate changing jibs, so long as all the sails are stored in rolled-up form, ready to hook on as soon as a newly-rolled sail has been taken down.

A Wykeham Martin jib furling gear can be of great benefit on a short-handed gaffer with a cutter foretriangle.

The only weakness of these systems is that they do not operate well in high winds, whether the sheet has been let fly or not. The answer is to run the boat off and roll away the jib in the calm spot behind the mainsail. This is usually easy enough to organise, so long as the skipper's tactical sense has not left him with no room to leeward for a quick 'furling job' while approaching a tight harbour in a blow.

JIB TOPSAILS

These sails are normally hanked onto the topmast forestay. They are sent aloft with a long tack strop which allows them to set as high as required. The sheets are led as far aft as possible. The function of a jib topsail is to slot air around the back of the main topsail, with the result that it produces far more power than its area would suggest. As has been noted in Chapter III, these sails are never hoisted without first setting up the weather topmast preventers.

One of the most powerful sails of all is the Yankee. This is really a full-hoist jib topsail which tacks down virtually to the bowsprit end. Its pull is simply phenomenal and it should be treated with the greatest respect. I remember running almost 40 miles through the water in a 4-hour watch aboard the 55ft cutter *Jolie Brise* with the Yankee pulling like a harpooned whale. I think we only had the bravado to do it because it was the middle watch, we were homeward bound, and it was too dark to see the topmast bending.....

The jib topsail
Note the tack strop, hanks and sheet led well aft.

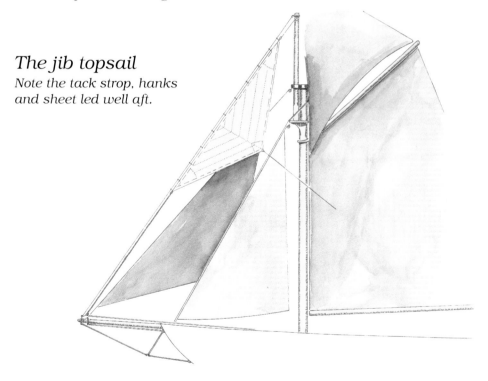

CHAPTER IX

MAKING THE RIG WORK

The foremost ingredient in making a boat perform 'up to snuff', is a skilfully cut suit of sails. Choose your sailmaker with care, and beware of glossy 'we do it all' advertising. The fact that a person can produce a first-class Bermudan mainsail is no guarantee that he or she can also cut a gaff sail that will deliver the goods. Looking around an average fleet of gaffers you'll see more poorly cut mainsails than handsome ones. Building the flow into a gaff sail is a specific technique, particularly the triangle that lies between the gaff and the leech, and a specialist sailmaker is best able to handle the question.

This is not to say that major lofts may not have someone on their books who knows how the job should be done. Just remember that cutting an individual type of sail is like playing a musical instrument: the more you do it, the better you become. Furthermore, someone who understands a gaff mainsail will usually design more suitable headsails to work with it, than one whose days are spent making genoas for high-aspect-ratio Bermudan boats.

The second item which has to be addressed before discussing sheeting angles and how close to the wind you should try to sail, is the matter of superfluous windage. We've already noted that baggywrinkle is to be used as a last resort to stop terminal chafe problems. We should now add that ratlines, lazy jacks, and extra purchases which look salty but are not strictly required, are all grouped under the heading of 'potential incubus'. Install them if you must, but remember that a 14mm line rigged 'up and down' exerts over a square foot of dead windage for every 12ft it goes aloft. Now consider the average dustbin lid of about 6 sq ft. Imagine what it would feel like trying to hold one at arm's length with its flat surface turned directly to face a gusty force 6 or 7. When that has been digested, calculate the area of your whole rig; mast, boom, gaff, ropes — the lot. You'll end up with a different point of view about anything that is not utterly vital, either to the business of generating wind power, or to ensuring that the whole contraption doesn't blow over the side in the process.

Before a boat moves a yard to windward, her sails must overcome the drag of all that windage. So keep the rig clean and sweet. The only thing a pilot cutter carried aloft that wasn't strictly necessary to her sailing was the pilot jack, but if she'd left that on deck she might as well have stayed on her mooring.

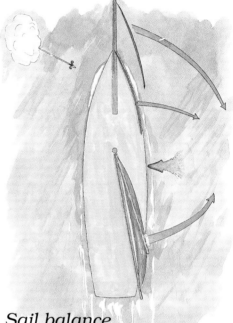

Sail balance

Any boat effectively pivots about her centre of lateral resistance. Any sail set abaft this tends to want to make her luff. Sail set forward makes her want to bear away. Balancing the two tendencies results in a light, neutral helm. Using one against the other can be a vital factor in close manoeuvres.

SHEETING ANGLES

On any boat, the only sail cutting clean air is the foremost one. In a gaff cutter, this must be the jib. As wind flows around the sail, its direction of travel is bent slightly. It is this which gives the sail its power.

The air flowing past the staysail has already been interfered with by the jib. In fact, its direction of flow has been distorted so that it is coming more from ahead than would otherwise have been the case. This means that if both jib and staysail are sheeted at the same angle to the centreline of the boat, the staysail luff will be backwinded by the air off the jib. This situation is obviously undesirable. It is avoided by sheeting the staysail in a little tighter.

By the time the air arrives at the mainsail, it has been bent still further, and the main is sheeted even harder to compensate, taking the topsail with it.

A sail generates its force approximately at right angles to a line joining luff and leech. If all things are equal, the greater the angle it is making with the boat's centre-line, the more forward push it is delivering. Its sideways effort is dissipated by the lateral resistance of the keel and by the heel of the boat. Maximum forward effort is extracted on a reach by easing the sheets until the sails are as far out as they will go without their luffs lifting*. On a reach, the jib is always adjusted first, because the air flowing off it affects all the other sails.

As a reach becomes broader, the sheets are progressively let off until the main boom comes up against the aft shrouds. At this point you can do no more, but because the sail is now delivering its message almost straight ahead, it is doing the best it can. Oversheeting sails on a broad reach is a common mistake in all sailing, not just on traditional craft, but it's notably unproductive with a large gaff mainsail. The tendency for a big main to build up weather helm is considerable. The further you are able to ease the sheet, therefore, the less will be the boat's desire to gripe to windward.

The same principles apply when a vessel is close-hauled. They are, however, applied more subtly, because the object of the exercise has altered. Reaching, the boat is steered towards her destination, and the sails are trimmed so as to give of their best. When she is close-hauled, her sails are set up to produce the optimum push commensurate with the boat lying as close to the wind as she realistically may; the helmsman then offers the whole boat, rig and all, to the airstream at such an angle that the wind blows correctly around the sails. If this ceases to happen, it is up to the helmsman, not the sheet hands, to bring the rig back into line with the wind; the only tool for achieving this end, is the tiller or wheel.

So how is the rig of a cutter to be set up for windward work?

1 — Bring all the sails in and commence sailing as close to the wind as you reasonably can on a 'guesstimate' of sail trim.

2 — Assuming there is a good sailing breeze, flatten in the staysail as hard as you can. This is the sail that determines how high you're going to point.

3 — Now trim the mainsail behind the staysail. Bear in mind that the further off the centre-line the boom is, the more forward drive the sail will offer. Even so, there is rarely any profit in allowing the main to lift more than a trifle.

4 — Oversheet the jib until it is drastically backwinding the staysail. As it does, the boat will slow down. Ease the jib sheet inch by inch until the staysail is just setting cleanly, and the boat accelerates again.

5 — Sail the boat so that the jib is not quite lifting.

6 — You are now as close to the wind as you can reasonably come without slowing down.

Obviously, there is no need to go through this procedure every time you tack. Once you know how things look, you'll be able to get it right instinctively with a few minor adjustments. The main thing to remember is that you are not operating a fin-keeled

Bermudan cruiser-racer. Very few gaffers will sail higher than 45° to the true wind, and many will in reality manage little better than 55°. Most will point higher than they will sail, but it rarely helps a boat's performance if her helmsman is greedy. If you oversheet the jib in order to stuff the boat up another half point onto the wind, she will slow down and make far more leeway than she was when sailing at her optimum angle.

Beating to windward

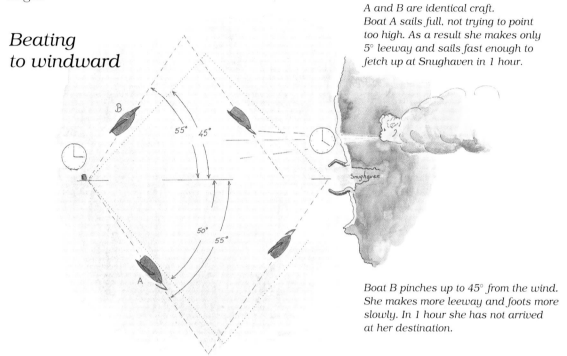

A and B are identical craft. Boat A sails full, not trying to point too high. As a result she makes only 5° leeway and sails fast enough to fetch up at Snughaven in 1 hour.

Boat B pinches up to 45° from the wind. She makes more leeway and foots more slowly. In 1 hour she has not arrived at her destination.

Vmg (Velocity made good to windward) is not only about pointing angle, it also concerns itself with boat speed through the water, and leeway. Beyond a certain critical value, the first is gained only by suffering terrible losses in the other two.

Dividends are earned in a seaway by coming off the wind a few degrees to power things up. Most gaffers have such a low aspect ratio rig, that so small a change in angle of attack will not involve you in easing the sheets. By opening the angle the wind is making with the sails, it will be bent more, and extra power will be generated. This does not happen with the taller, narrower Bermudan rig, where any change of direction must be accompanied by a corresponding trimming of the sheets.

So far in this chapter we have talked about the cutter. The same principles apply to simpler rigs, as well as those of greater complexity. In all conscience, however, I cannot sign off this section without confessing that when it comes to schooners, those mystic vessels, this logical, almost scientific approach to sail trim can be laid low by the intuition of a master.

One time, I was racing aboard the *Brilliant*, in Fishers Island Sound, Connecticut. We were reaching at 9½ knots in a fine beam wind under every stitch we could carry.

'Well, mister', the skipper had noticed me peering at his rig, 'do you reckon you can get any more out of her?'

I had been convinced for some time that the mainsail was oversheeted.

'Mind if I try?'

He'd seen what I was thinking, before I spoke. 'Go ahead', he said inscrutably.

There was a serious amount of weight in that mainsheet, but I kept a couple of turns on and carefully eased it. I must have let out 10ft before the luff of the main twitched, then I found two strong men to help me pull it back in a foot or two.

'How's that?' I enquired, convinced we would be better off.

In his youth on the Grand Banks the skipper had learned that gestures are more eloquent than words. By way of reply, he jerked his head towards the digital log and the wind instruments. The wind speed was exactly the same. Our speed had fallen by ¼ knot.

We pulled the sail back to his fancy and stormed away at 9½ once more. 'There are more things in heaven and earth, my son...'

TWIST

Up to now, our discussion of sheeting angles has been about how far to pull the sails in or let them out. There is a different aspect to sheeting, however, which is not given nearly so much consideration in gaff rig as in modern craft. This is the matter of where the sheet leads are to be positioned.

Any boat today which makes a pretence to performance, sports fully adjustable sheet leads to control the leech tension of her sails. Headsail leads move fore and aft on tracks, mainsheets slide athwartships by means of a traveller. On gaffers, such refinements are rarely available. This will always seem a shame to those of us used to the benefits these alterations bring, but if the boat in question is an original, we are generally beneficiaries of gear left to us by our predecessors, whether we like it or not. Indeed, to bolt a genoa track onto the deck of a Lowestoft smack or a Maine schooner would be a crime against sensitive humanity.

We can make small adjustments to the headsail sheeting angle by raising and lowering the whole sail on a tack strop, but the only really satisfactory method is to cut the sail to the position of the fairlead. The sheet angle to the clew should then be such that if continued in a straight line, the rope would meet the luff about 35% of the way up. If the sail is mitre-cut, the lead will meet the luff slightly above the mitre. Where this end is achieved, the headsails should give full power. If the sheet lead is too far aft, the top of the sail falls off the wind, or twists, excessively. Wind will be spilled from the upper portion, which will be seen to luff, even when close-hauled. If the lead is too far forward, the upper leech will hook to windward, causing that part of the sail to stall as though it were oversheeted.

Twist in a mainsail/topsail combination is more dramatic than in headsails, and more can be done to control it.

Main and topsail twist under perfect control aboard Solweig.

A certain amount of twist is desirable here for two reasons: as the boat sails along, she generates what is in effect a headwind equal and opposite to her own speed. This is not felt directly, but it has the effect of pulling the true wind further forward, to form the apparent wind in which the boat is actually sailing. The greater the discrepancy between the true wind speed and the boat speed, the less the interference resulting in apparent wind. Therefore, since the wind aloft is stronger than at deck level, the wind up there is not pulled forward so much as the breeze lower down, and the upper part of the sail can be allowed to set further from the boat's centre-line.

Secondly, of course, unless a jib topsail is carried, the upper part of the main and the topsail are cutting air almost as undisturbed as that of the jib. In consequence, their wind is freer than that which blows over the lower section of the sail, because down there it has been bent by the headsails.

All this is highly convenient, because a certain amount of twist is endemic in the rig. The problem is usually to prevent it from becoming out of hand. On a ketch, or a schooner's foremast, this is easily achieved by rigging a gaff vang through a block on the mizzen (or schooner's mainmast) and adjusting it from down on deck. Fine control is possible by this means.

A friend of mine has a gaff vang rigged on his cutter, and has successfully circumnavigated twice with the arrangement. He swears by it, not only as a means of minimising twist, but also because by effectively sheeting the gaff as well as the boom when reaching, he can check the wild swinging which often occurs on the ocean and causes a devilish amount of chafe. In spite of this testimonial, it must be said that few cutters rig vangs, because finding an advantageous lead is extremely difficult.

The other way of controlling twist in a gaff sail is to heave down vertically on the boom end. A heavy boom does much of this work for itself, while a horse of the type employed by the Colin Archer in Chapter II allows the sheet to pull directly downwards when close-hauled. If a boat is fitted with a turning block on each quarter to enable the mainsheet to be handled from either side, twist can sometimes be reduced by heaving down on the lee part of the sheet. Theoretically, this should not work, as both parts of the sheet should even up, but in reality, friction does its work and some of the twist can be pulled out.

TACKING AND GYBING

Running backstays

Whenever a boat is to be tacked or gybed, both runners should be set up for a second or so, rather than letting one off before the other comes on. This makes the mast more secure, and the job less strenuous. If one runner is already on, the only effort required to tension the other is to take up the slack. If you are starting from scratch, you have to work against the pull of the headsails. Moreover, if you have Highfield levers, you may well find them impossible to turn once the load is on the rig. One day, I tried to force a small, delicate lever on with my foot. It buckled, and the message was clear: 'if something won't work that ought to be working, don't force it; engage brain, and find out what's wrong.' The advice runs true throughout all seafaring.

Steering through a tack

In some ways, it's easier to tack a traditional gaffer than a modern sloop with no forefoot at all. The reason is time. Because of her hull shape, a long-keeled craft tacks steadily. This offers ample opportunity to sheet in the headsails before the wind fills them, even if there are no winches. Those misguided enough to design gaff-rigged craft with no forefoot are throwing away this advantage, along with several other vital gains.

1 — First, make sure the boat is sailing as fast as she can, then tack her smartly.

2 — The headsail sheets are not let off until the sails are lifting positively. Slack is gathered on the new lee sheets as she passes through stays, then both headsails are sheeted in board flat before the boat has turned more than 30° from the wind. There should be plenty of time for this, so long as the sheets are conveniently accessible and no one steps on your hand.

3 — When the boat has filled on the new tack, the jib sheet is eased until the right setting is found. A jib topsail or a Yankee is treated just the same. We have discussed running backstays on the previous page.

You'll notice that there is no talk here of backing headsails 'to get her round'. In a good boat, properly sailed, this is rarely necessary. Occasionally, if she is grossly overcanvassed, or if the head sea is abnormally steep, it will help to hold the staysail aback until you are confident she'll make it, but this should be the exception rather than the rule. In calm water, backing a headsail is counter-productive because although it ensures a successful tack, it also puts the foretriangle into 'reverse drive'. Since we in gaff-rigged craft have so little to give away when working to windward, it seems tragic to sacrifice anything at all.

If your boat is showing a tendency to miss stays in strong winds, it may be that her main or mizzen is oversheeted. This will help her to come up into the wind, but if she is losing a lot of way as she comes round, it will also stop her falling onto the new tack. Try easing the mizzen sheet (or mainsheet) a few feet as she comes through the wind, then bringing it back on as speed builds up once more.

A boat whose bottom is less than clean will be far more likely to misbehave as she tacks. Brixham trawler ketches have been known to heave the mizzen boom up to windward in the initial stages of a tack to help shove the stern down to leeward when carrying a garden of weed.

A final word about missing stays: if you do become stuck head-to-wind and begin sailing backwards, it may not be enough just to back your headsail and hope for the best. Once you begin making sternway, your rudder steers in reverse just as though you were manoeuvring under power. If you leave it where it was during the tack which failed, it will be working against your staysail as this tries to pull your head round. Reverse your helm though, and she'll fall off like a lady.

Gybing

If you have runners, never let them be far from your consciousness, particularly when a gybe is on the cards, whether voluntary or involuntary.

Many working seamen habitually gybed all standing*, and never gave the matter a thought. However, their craft had massive buffer arrangements on the mainsheet blocks. These served the dual purpose of absorbing the shock of a heavy gybe, as well as the constant snatching of the boom in light weather at sea. You need nerves of steel to follow their example, even if your gear may seem up to it.

By far the safest way to gybe is to put your best helmsman on the tiller, then run dead downwind while the mainsheet is hauled close aboard and both runners are set up. When the sheet is in, a turn is taken and the new lee runner is let off. The helm is now put up and the sail gybes. As it does so the helm balance will suddenly change, so unless you want to screw up to windward in a hurry by 30° or so, the 'driver' should apply 'opposite helm' to correct the tendency. At the same time, the sheet hands are easing away for all they are worth. If it's really blowing, they will have to be smart about it, otherwise in all but the most directionally stable of craft the helmsman will have a struggle maintaining control.

Don't worry about the headsails. Unless they are poled out, they will cause no problems and can be gybed separately after the main event. If they are poled out, consult Chapter XIII. There is only one thing to remember when gybing a headsail: always take up the slack on the new sheet before releasing the old. If you don't do this, sooner or later the sail will fly out round the forestay. This isn't a catastrophe, but it is untidy and unnecessary.

❂❂❂❂❂❂❂❂❂

CHAPTER X

SHORTENING SAIL

It would be idle to pretend that reducing canvas in a gaff-rigged craft is a less complicated process than in her Bermudan equivalent. Even a small gaffer has more strings to pull. The mainsail is considerably larger. There are hankless jibs to be fought and topsails to be tamed. Indeed, only staysails appear on the bill of fare as simple sails to handle. Brute force and ignorance are no help. Tackled properly and early, however, there isn't a sail on the boat which need cause any problems.

Unlike life on the roads, where motor cars plummet towards one another at mind-boggling speeds, the sea will always allow us a few moments to think, if it gets a chance. This is particularly true where long-keeled traditional craft are concerned. They are by nature so steady on their feet that if they are handled sympathetically, time will always be on your side. This facet of their character becomes important when you have to shorten sail. The last thing you want on a rough night is to be hanging over the vessel's quarter as she surges along, scrabbling at the end of the boom for reef pendants. To do so is frightening, counter-productive and unnecessary. On this, and most other occasions where life is becoming hectic, the situation can be instantly defused by the simple expedient of heaving-to.

HEAVING-TO

It is rarely absolutely necessary to heave-to when shortening sail, but in tough going it can make the difference between trauma and a low-stress, workmanlike job.

Unlike a flat-floored, fin-keeled yacht, a heavy-displacement gaffer heaves to superbly. With her head tucked under her wing, her motion is eased dramatically, and she can be trimmed to drift slowly across the wind, making little or no leeway. Her deck becomes a safe and agreeable place to work, so that the task in hand can be tackled with the confidence that you will have the same number of crew when you finish as when you began.

The Mechanics of Heaving-to

The stability of the hove-to state relies on the fact that any sail forward of the vessel's centre of lateral resistance tends to swivel her head away from the wind, while anything set aft will do the same for the stern. If both chunks of sail area are sheeted to deliver their drive in a forward direction, they balance one another. The boat can then move ahead with any minor deviations being compensated by her rudder.

If the boat is placed with the wind well forward of the beam and the headsails sheeted aback, she will lose all way and her bow will tend to fall off the wind. This continues until she is sufficiently beam-on for the mainsail to fill. At this point she will try to drive ahead. As long as her helm* is lashed down so that her rudder lies to windward, the mainsail will not drive for any length of time because both it and the rudder will induce the boat to point up towards the wind. The main then loses power and the backed headsails push the bow off again. And so on.

In theory, any vessel will 'gill and fill' like this indefinitely. In practice, many short-keeled yachts find it impossible to remain quiet. They either tack themselves out of the hove-to mode, or lie uncomfortably with the wind on, or even abaft the beam. A gaff-rigged boat with a deep forefoot will adopt an equilibrium with her bow somewhere between 30° and 60° from the wind. The seas may knock her around, but she will sort herself out without any help from her crew and quickly settle down once more.

The best way to heave-to in a boat with no winches is to bring her onto a close reach, then come about without casting off the headsail sheets. When she is through the wind and the headsails are well aback, the helm is lashed down to leeward. This accomplishes the business with a minimum of hauling and grunting, but does involve you in a change of tack.

If you want to remain on the same tack, you will have to haul the headsails across to the weather side before lashing the helm down. This can be a serious pull. It is easily avoided, however, by running the boat off the wind for a short while so as to take the weight off the headsail sheets. While they are in the mainsail's wind shadow, both sails are close-hauled onto the weather side. When the sheets have been made up, the boat is brought to the wind, the mainsheet hauled well in, and the helm lashed down.

As soon as the world has become a more peaceful place, you can start reefing down.

REEFING A GAFF SAIL

Having preached the gospel of heaving-to for reefing, I find myself having to note yet again that everything must be settled up for in the end. By definition, a yacht which is hove-to spends most of her time with the mainsail full of wind, even if the canvas is not strictly driving. The muscle-work of reefing is actually eased if the main is spilling wind. On balance, a certain amount of extra effort for the minute or so that you spend pulling down the clew cringle pays off many times over on the rest of the job.

The reefing procedure in a classic, points-reefing mainsail goes as follows: everything is included here as though the sail were of 500sq ft or more. A smaller area of canvas will be controlled with less work on the purchases.

1 — Top up the boom; use the weather lift if there is a choice.

2 — Overhaul the throat halyard purchase so that its full length will be available when required.

3 — Ease the throat halyard carefully until the first tack reefing cringle is close to the main tack cringle. Make fast the halyard.

4 — If there is no permanently rigged tack pendant, bend a length of strong lashing to the reef cringle with a fisherman's bend. Now lash down the tack. It might suit you to lash the two cringles together, or you may prefer to lash the reef cringle down to the boom goose neck. If the sail is loose-footed with a tack downhaul, you have only to hook this to the reef cringle and haul away until the tack is at the height you want.

5 — Tension up the luff of the sail using the throat halyard purchase.

6 — Hook the outboard block of the reefing tackle to the relevant reefing pendant (see Chapter VI), and pull down the clew. If the geometry of the sail is ideal, you will be able to take in one or even two reefs without any adjustment to the peak halyard, other than minor trimming dealt with by the purchase. Many sails do not have this feature, and it then becomes necessary to ease the peak halyard before attempting to pull down the clew cringle.

Even if a sail can normally be reefed without attention to the peak, easing the halyard will help the job along in a hard blow. The only trouble is, once the peak halyard has been let off it will have to be set up again afterwards, which involves more sweat and rope coiling.

7 — With tack and clew cringles on the boom, it only remains to tie up the reef points. You could circumnavigate with a modern Bermudan sail and never bother with the points at all. For the long, low gaff sail, this is not on the cards. If the sail is rigged with individual reefing ties, you should now pass these under the foot of the sail, heave them up tight, and tie them off with a reef knot. Don't tie them round the boom because that could put too much strain on the cloth in way of the reefing points. You might prefer to 'slip' the second half-hitch like a shoe-lace bow so that it can be more easily released.

One benefit of a loose-footed sail is its facility for tying off the reef points. Standing in perfect safety between the boom and the sail, you can gather up the cloth of the foot with the ties. If the sail is laced to the boom your task is to pull a sail half-full of wind right up to the woodwork, which can be extremely hard work in a heavy vessel. By the time you get to the final reef in a gale it will certainly be a two-man job on each point.

An alternative system is the use of a lacing to tie up the reef. On the positive side this ensures that the load is evenly distributed between all the eyelets along the sail. It is also quick to let go when you are ready to shake out the reef. These two features made the method popular with racing yachts. Unfortunately, the lacing is generally impractical in a short-handed cruising boat. The logistical problems of threading a long lacing around the foot of a large lump of wet sail in the darkness outweigh its beneficial features. It is far easier to work with individual points.

On a big sail with a full crew, it is better when tying up the points to start at both

↑ *Lace reefing is kind to the sail, but is not generally otherwise desirable aboard an offshore cruiser.*
← *Neatly reefed to balance her in the gusts, this little sloop is enjoying an easy ride.*

ends of the boom and work towards the middle. It is the ties in the central third that are taking most strain. If you work towards these, most of the wind has been 'tied out' of the reefed part of the sail when you reach the heaviest ones.

8 — Traditionally, when this stage has been reached, one is supposed to lash the clew cringle tightly to the boom, then ease the reefing tackle. With modern ropes, there is really no need for this, except possibly in the largest vessels when desperate weather is expected. It is always awkward to reach the clew, and to tie in the lashing could be dangerous. I have never found it necessary to lash the clew on a boom whose pendant leads are good, even on long ocean legs.

9 — When the reef is securely tied in, take up the slack in the topsail sheet and ensign halyard if they are rigged. Also, pull through the slack in the pendants for any reefs not yet used, and tie them off somewhere on the boom. If you don't, they will trail in the water. They may also seize the opportunity to garrotte the helmsman as the boat comes through the wind, especially when she gybes.

10 — If you had to ease the peak halyard, now is the time to set it up again. Doing this before tying in the reef would make that job even harder. When the boat has a long peak purchase (a highly desirable feature) and you have been circumspect about how much halyard you originally eased away, the purchase will take care of the whole task. Heaving the gaff back up with the hauling part of the halyard can be such hard work, you may begin to wish you'd never bothered.

11 — Ease the topping lift, coil down, tidy up, lay aft, and start sailing again. The whole job will take one person about 10 minutes in a 32ft cutter. In a 50-footer, two or three people will be needed if the task is to be completed in the same time.

12 — For further reefs, repeat the procedure. If you're caught out with far too much canvas set, you can take two reefs for the price of one, by going straight for the second reef cringles and missing the first out altogether. The only draw-back is that you'll have a jolly session tying in the points.

Shaking out reefs

Perhaps it is because conditions are calming down, or maybe it is purely the psychology of the situation, but whatever the reason, one rarely feels the need to heave-to in order to shake out a reef. It can usually be done comfortably enough while sailing along.

If the sail is squared off, you'll have to pull in the sheet to bring the job within range. Now support the boom on the topping lift, untie the points, release the tack and clew cringles, ease the sheet so that the sail is spilling wind, and hoist away. Don't forget to slack up on the topsail sheet, otherwise you'll wonder why the sail won't go back up again. Most ensign halyards are of light material and may well part if you ignore them while you haul on the peak purchase. One of my boats had an ensign halyard belayed on a neat little cleat screwed to the side of the boom. I often wished I had a pound for every time I pulled it off.

Always keep a close eye on what your crew are up to when shaking out reefs. It's all too easy for an inexperienced hand to let go the clew pendant before the ties have been undone. If this were to happen on a heavy boat and you'd forgotten to make up the topping lift, sail damage would be a certainty.

One final word about shaking out reefs: because the peak is up when you start to re-hoist, you may have a struggle with the throat halyard. The difficulty you are experiencing indicates that you are fighting the geometry of the rig, rather than letting it work for you. In consequence, you are not only risking internal injury, you are also putting excess strain on your gear. The only solution is to ease the peak away until the gaff is nearly parallel with the boom. The throat will become comparatively light, and even if you are left with a hard pull on the peak, you'll know the rig is not being damaged.

Roller Reefing

Because luff and leech are more nearly parallel, particularly in a ketch, roller reefing works more tidily and is easier to use on a gaff than a Bermudan sail. Regardless of its type, a roller-reefed sail never sets as sweetly as one shortened down conventionally. Nevertheless, the system was adopted by many Bristol Channel pilots, who felt that the resulting decreased driving efficiency was an acceptable compromise for an ability to reef the main single-handed.

In these vessels the process of reefing proceeds as follows:

1 — Heave-to, if this seems desirable.

2 — Top up the boom.

3 — Ease the throat halyard a few feet at a time and take up the slack by rolling the sail around the boom.

4 — The equivalent of two reefs can sometimes be taken without touching the peak halyard. If more than this are required, the peak will need to be eased.

5 — When the desired amount of canvas has been rolled away, the peak halyard can be set up if necessary on the purchase, the topping lift eased, and the boat got under way again.

Some people prefer to roller reef with wind in the sail, others will swear that a neat reef can only be achieved by luffing the sail 'onto the shake'. Find out by experiment what your boat likes best, but whatever you do, raise the boom end well up on the topping lift. This stops the boom from drooping when you ease the halyards, and prevents the luff-rope of the sail from creeping forward to foul the roller gear.

Roller reefing gears must be kept well lubricated, particularly the swivelling sheet bail at the boom end. If that fails to work on a black night, the first you'll know about it is when you try to slack away on the mainsheet and discover it inextricably tangled around the boom.

The Appledore patent reefing gear aboard a Bristol Channel Pilot Cutter.

Don't fight the boat

The question of reefing brings out the art rather than the science of sailing a gaffer. If you have winches for many of the jobs, the whole process will be painless, but the very power of the winch may encourage you to overstress a piece of gear which you would be unable to damage by traditional means. So watch out. If you have no winches, try to make the movement of the boat work for you, rather than against you.

For example, pulling down the clew pendant is usually the hardest task of all, unless you are going to let off the peak far beyond what would otherwise be desirable. If you are hove-to, from time to time the boat will luff sufficiently to shake the mainsail. Wait for that moment, be ready, then when the sail spills its wind, take it unawares and whack its clew down before it knows what hit it.

Use the roll of the boat to assist your rope-swigging, and above all, if something doesn't want to come, take the trouble to investigate. You can heave away if you have the muscle. If you haven't, you'll need to work things out. Gaff rig is so flexible that there's always another way of tackling a task. Find it, and your life will be sweet.

Coming out of the hove-to condition

One technique for getting under way after being hove-to is to let draw the headsails, centralise the helm, and sail off. However, if it's blowing hard and you've no sheet winches, such an action is unlikely to endear a skipper to his crew, particularly if his next step is to go about.

If you do need to change tack you can always destroy the hove-to equilibrium by putting the helm up. A well-balanced boat should then continue to turn off the wind until she gybes round onto the new tack. As she comes through the breeze, the boom will be controlled because it is already sheeted in. The headsails will flop quietly across. The only work involved is shoving the tiller over.

A less perfectly balanced craft, or perhaps one which still has her topsail set (or has just re-set it), may refuse to bear away until you ease the mainsheet some distance. You probably won't have to let off much and it will be easy to snaffle it back, if required, as the boat gybes.

Reefing with the sail on deck

Putting a reef into the sail before setting out on a windy day is an obvious precaution. The trouble is, reefing with the sail on deck is always a messy business. Nothing ever seems to line up, and I, for one, always tie at least one reef point around the topsail sheet, or perform some other nonsense which only shows itself when the sail is hoisted.

For this reason, any temptation to drop the sail at sea to reef it should be resisted vigorously. A substantial vessel of my acquaintance had such inadequate reefing gear that it was impossible to take a tuck without dropping the whole sail. One passage was enough.

REEFING STAYSAILS

Unlike a gaff main, mizzen or foresail, a staysail is usually best reefed down on deck. By the time you are thinking about shortening its area, conditions are usually harsh, not to say severe, so it is always preferable to heave-to under main and jib while you execute the task. This won't be possible on a sloop, so you'll have to manage as best you can, though as with all operations on the foredeck, running off carefully to shadow the sail and decrease the apparent wind will help.

It is possible to contrive a reef with the sail either drawing or aback, by first transferring the lazy sheet to the new clew, taking the load on it, and shifting the working sheet while the weight is off. At this stage, the sail will look rather odd and will be suffering untoward strains, so the tack must now be reefed quickly. Tying in the points is no problem on a staysail as the area is small and there is nothing to resist your efforts.

Some sloops and cutters carry two or three reefs in their staysails. These may all be rigged with points, but often only the first reef is thus provided, for the sake of convenience. The deeper reefs are tied in with a short lacing.

Reefing the staysail can ease a vessel's head wonderfully.

COMBINATIONS OF REDUCED SAIL

It doesn't matter what boat you are sailing, the effects of being over-canvassed are two-fold. First, she heels further than either she or her crew wants. Secondly, most boats develop additional weather helm as they heel. This is partly a result of the changing hull form which is immersed. A boat's lines may be well balanced when she is floating upright, but once she is heeled, her good manners often deteriorate. This phenomenon is prevalent in certain modern flat-floored cruisers. Gaffers are not generally beamy, but those that are, such as Colin Archers, are of superior design to today's performance and accommodation oriented flyers, so helm imbalance from heeling alone is not such a serious problem. Nevertheless, the weight on the tiller will increase with the wind, particularly when broad reaching in a vessel with a long boom. In this case the imbalance is caused by the fact that the centre of effort of the mainsail is far out over the side of the boat. The rudder alone can compensate for this, and weather helm is the inevitable result.

By the time heeling or weather helm have become a nuisance, it is already somewhat late to be reefing down. When you know your boat, you'll be aware of the subtle signs which precede this state, but in any case, the rule of thumb is always comfort for helmsman, crew or both. Nine times out of ten, if a reef is taken at the right moment the boat will not slow down. She may even go faster, and the peace of mind for the skipper thinking about his gear will be well worth the effort.

The only exception to the general philosophy of reefing early comes when working to windward. The boat has yet to be built that doesn't need driving to weather. After all, it's not a natural thing to do. Sailing an elderly boat hard to windward in a seaway always hurts a sensitive seaman. This probably doesn't cause the vessel as much pain as he imagines and if he wants her to live up to her performance potential, it must be done. In spite of this logic, most of us don't really enjoy it, and that is where the new yacht built on traditional lines comes into her own.

All this must be borne in mind when deciding which sails to bring in, and in what order. Contrary to general impressions, a ketch is often best served by dropping her mizzen early rather than late, because it creates more weather helm than the main, and is often less solidly stayed. For the same reason, a schooner will reef her main before her foresail. In most gaffers, however, the topsails come off first. It is easier to drop a topsail, even a yard topsail, than to reef a mainsail, and the capacity these active little items have for creating havoc, if left up too long, provides motivation in plenty.

This ketch is making an easy ride of 25 knots of breeze under headsails and mizzen.

After the topsail, any large headsails such as genoas or balloon staysails come in, to be replaced with working jib and staysail. A gaffer under lower working canvas becomes comparatively easy to operate. The next reduction in a cutter will be a reef in the mainsail, followed by a second reef, if there are more than two.

When the main is reefed and the drama still increases, it is time for a reduction in headsail area. Initially, this is most effectively achieved by changing down to a smaller jib. Nowadays, most craft carry a maximum of three, so at this stage you may be going for the smallest, or spitfire jib.

There are two benefits in getting the jib down to minimum size before conditions become hectic. The first is that the jib is the liveliest sail on board and the longer you leave it, the more exciting it will be to change. The second is that a jib delivering too much power will bury the boat's bows when sailing to windward. The same is true to a lesser extent of the staysail, so the next reduction, if the wind is forward of the beam, will be a reef in that.

My own boat is not heavily canvassed for her tonnage, and she enjoys the advantage for deep-sea work of retaining her original mast and boom. Her rig is therefore as nature intended it to be. Going to windward at sea in force 6, she will have two reefs in the main and will, ideally, be down to her small jib. Depending upon sea state, she may also have the first reef down in her staysail. To carry more canvas than that merely over-presses her. She goes no faster, and all hands have a rougher, wetter ride.

Off the wind is a different story. If you are crazy enough and can keep her going straight, any well balanced craft will bear as much sail as you think her masts will stand. In the immortal words of that Yankee skipper, the late Captain Resolution Godworthy, 'What she can't carry, she can drag!' Nonetheless, if you find yourself transported by your own enthusiasm, never forget that if it blows another 5 knots, you'll have to get some canvas off her before the rig gives up the struggle and does the job for you.

In the worst of weather, most vessels whose rig sports a 'cutter' foretriangle will jog along merrily under deep-reefed main (or trysail, see chapter XI) and double-reefed staysail. Performance won't be anything to shout about, but the mast certainly won't go over the side. Your only worry will be whether or not you'll make port before the towels go up on the beer pumps.

HEAVY WEATHER

There are various ways of defining heavy weather. For our purposes, however, the most comprehensive statement would be that it is the sort of conditions which cause a vessel at sea to change her passage plan, or one in harbour to decide not to venture out.

You'll notice that this definition makes no attempt to name specific wind forces. This is because one vessel's heavy weather could be merely a hard sailing breeze for another. A 20-footer faced with a slog to windward in force 6 is experiencing heavy weather. A 70ft schooner would shape up to the same challenge with relish.

Similarly, a 32ft boat on a broad reach in force 7 might be feeling the wind, but not be truly inconvenienced by it, yet if her course placed the same breeze forward of the beam her crew might be inclined to go somewhere else instead. 'Her crew', notice. Heavy weather is not purely a matter of the vessel herself, it is also decided by her crew's strength, and their inclination to put her to the test.

The question of sea state is sometimes more important than wind strength. A well-found 40-footer can go yachting in force 8 in sheltered water; in a gale at sea, her crew would probably be wishing they were in the Bar du Port instead. It is waves which make the difference. Waves are the ogres that savage boats, it is rarely wind alone.

Although it is more burdensome to handle than a Bermudan rig, a well-found gaff rig copes with heavy weather at least as capably as its triangular equivalent. The low stresses and generally massive nature of gaff rig mean that vital components are less likely to carry away. The sail area, spread right along the boat's length and beyond to the bowsprit, supplies leverage at both ends when required, or can be snugged down inboard for safety if it is not.

The conclusive gain over the modern yacht, however, is the innate sea-kindliness of the traditional hull forms. They are stable on the helm, and the long-keeled craft with a deep forefoot is always able to look after herself in a blow. This is the final balance to set off against the superior speed of the more up-to-date profiles, both to windward and in light airs. It is nothing short of tragic to see ill-informed designers creating gaffers which have their underwater profile cut drastically away. The seakeeping capacity of such a boat, particularly a smallish one, will be seriously compromised, while the necessary limitations of the rig will not permit full advantage to be taken of the hull.

Gaff rig and heavy displacement go hand in hand. If you want to survive hard weather without a large crew, they form a combination that still has not been beaten.

SPARS

In the past, it was customary for fully-crewed vessels with topmasts to strike them at sea in preparation for storm conditions. The technique for raising and lowering these spars has been discussed in Chapter III. The effect on stability of removing so much weight from so high up must be dramatic, but I confess that I have never carried out this exercise myself, nor do I know anyone who has.

Generally speaking, the topmast was not brought right down to the deck, for the obvious reason that threading it back up through its spectacle irons* in a seaway would have been discouraging to say the least. Instead, it was sent down far enough for its cap just to engage in at least one of the fittings, and its heel was lashed against the lower spar. The length of the sort of topmast which would have received this treatment was such that its weight would sometimes be supported by the deck itself.

Running the bowsprit inboard also has a beneficial effect on the boat's ability to ride the sea. Her tendency to pitch will be much reduced by bringing so great a mass closer to the boat's centre of gravity. If the bowsprit runs, therefore, and jibs are no longer required due to press of weather, the boat will be better off if it is brought aboard.

Topmast is housed (still in spectacle iron, with heel lashed at goose-neck) and bowsprit run inboard. She will sail well enough on a reach under staysail and reefed mizzen, although her performance to windward will be comparatively poor.

A ketch snugged down for a hard blow

Tying in the last few reef points may be more trouble than it is worth. The sail is under control — looks perfectly seamanlike.

SAILS

Sails ought to become less full as they are reefed down. The smaller sails, such as number two and three jibs, should be cut flatter than the larger number ones they replace. This is because at higher windspeeds a flatter sail can generate all the power it needs. A full-cut sail will tend to be overpowered in strong winds; even if it is not, it will be more difficult to sheet, and will create an inordinate amount of drag. It will also increase heeling and, as a consequence, weather helm.

Except when trying to work to windward in extremis, it is always worth shortening sail in good time. More than once, I have found myself in the embarrassing position of being physically unable to pull the deep reef into a big gaff main, simply because I had left it too late. On one occasion off the coast of Greenland, we ended up with the choice of dropping it, or losing it. We opted for the former, but the half hour or so needed for the job afforded ample leisure for reflecting on our folly. If we'd reefed twenty minutes earlier we'd have been finished in ten minutes, with all hands turned in. As it was, we were grateful to secure the boom on deck, then more or less tame the freezing canvas and the homicidal gaff without anyone being knocked over the side.

Trysails

In the golden age of gaff, large racing yachts were often rigged with mainsails and topsails of such enormous proportions that they were not a serious proposition for passage-making. When voyaging from one regatta to the next, those huge areas of canvas were substituted by trysails of half the mainsail size, or less. These sails were like miniature mainsails, setting from short gaffs, but they were usually boomless. In all normal sailing breezes, they drove the sweet-lined hulls adequately, so that many excellent passage times were recorded, including a number of transatlantic voyages by *America*'s Cup challengers.

In winter, working vessels set trysails of a similar nature. The great mainsails of the North American fishing schooners were a source of embarrassment when they were engaged on the Banks. Handling the 80ft main boom was an all-hands job, and since at such times most of the men were away in the dories, a trysail solved their problems.

The traditional trysail was set from a short gaff, with the usual main and throat halyards. This might seem a lot of unnecessary work and complication, but there is little doubt that such sails produced far more drive than the 'thimble-headed' or 'leg-of-mutton' trysails of today. These have replaced the old-fashioned ones for the simple reason that no one wants to cart an extra gaff around with them, on the off-chance that one day they might need it. A 3-cornered trysail, especially a small one, is not a lot of use when attempting to work to windward, even for a modern sloop. With a good storm jib and a well-setting reefed staysail, it will see you away from a lee shore, but I haven't yet operated a gaffer that would point up more than 65° from the wind under such a sail.

The greatest advantage of a trysail over a deep-reefed main is that the boom and gaff are stowed, ideally down on deck, or at least on a short crutch or a gallows. This relieves the mast, and hence the boat, of the strain of their weight. The trysail is set with two sheets, one each side, so the boom becomes entirely redundant.

With modern sailcloth the trysail enjoys another useful feature; it is always 'fresh out of the bag'. It sees so little use that the polyester cloth undergoes virtually no degradation from sailcloth-munching ultraviolet light. It is therefore not going to blow out, however hard the gale. In the bad old days of natural fibre, a sail which was often perforce stowed wet, then left for months in its clammy bag, was prone to rot.

Trysails are generally attached to the mast with toggles on the ends of parrel lines. The tack is spliced into a downhaul which enables its height above the stowed gaff to be adjusted. Most trysails are set up towards the hounds. This keeps them clear of any interference to the wind by the waves, as well as offering a variety of sheet lead angles.

The easiest system for bending the sail on at sea is to always bag it so that the luff, with its two ends prominent, is immediately available on releasing the drawstring. You can then tie the bag to the mast and attach the whole business edge, before the wind gets a look at the rest of the sail. When you're ready, hook on the halyard, find the

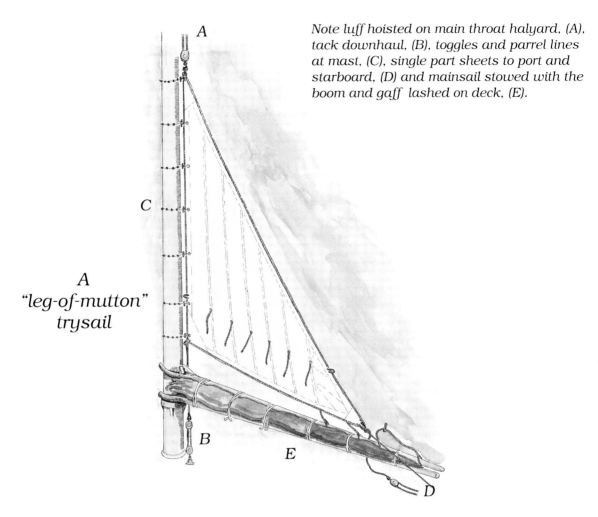

Note luff hoisted on main throat halyard, (A), tack downhaul, (B), toggles and parrel lines at mast, (C), single part sheets to port and starboard, (D) and mainsail stowed with the boom and gaff lashed on deck, (E).

A
"leg-of-mutton"
trysail

clew and make fast the lee sheet loosely, whip the bag away, then hoist immediately. If the baggers have let you down you'll have to keep the sail from flogging by lying on it while you toggle up and bend on the tack. Beware of the flailing sheets as you hoist. They are the devil manifest.

Even if you are unimpressed with the windward performance of your trysail, it is of great value on a long reach in tough going. As the gale abates, you can power things up with the headsails until the sea has gone down sufficiently to tackle the main boom. The trysail is also a useful ally when you anticipate an extended spell hove-to, especially if you fear the wind will harden still further. The boat may not 'look up' quite so well as she does with her main set, but your peace of mind will be complete, as you lie in your bunk hour after hour, waiting for the cold front to herald an improvement.

Dropping the mainsail in a blow at sea

This is a totally different experience from the well-planned procedure we all go through, head-to-wind, in a nice, calm harbour. With luck, you'll have all the reefs in before it becomes obvious that the sail has to come down. If anything more than its minimum area is showing, so much the worse for you.

The problem is to persuade the boat to point sufficiently close to the wind to allow the sail to shake until you can get it down. You may feel that you can drop the sail without it having to spill wind, but in a serious gale you could be unlucky. If you are fully crewed, you can gather as much way as possible, then luff almost, but not quite, head to wind. The boat should carry her way for long enough to allow you to do the job. Shorthanded, though, you'll need to manage without a helmsman, because all hands will be required to jump on the gaff when it hits the deck. The method expounded below works from a hove-to state. The chances are you'll be hove-to with your jib stowed by now anyway. If not, do it.

1 — Top up the boom.

2 — Overhaul your halyard purchases.

3 — If you have a crutch or gallows and you can manage to persuade the boom onto it (you may have to ease some more peak halyard), do it now, and double-lash it. Never mind if you haven't, just haul the mainsheet in as tight as you can get it.

4 — Flake both halyards so that they have no opportunity whatever to foul. Then secure the bitter ends so that come what may, you cannot lose the halyards aloft. If the seas wash them off the deck, keep trying. Sooner or later your chance will come.

5 — Take up the slack on the lee-side staysail sheet. Prepare the windward one for release.

6 — Feed your sail ties over the boom ready for action, and have some spares in your pockets or round your waist in case they all blow away.

7 — Make sure the helm is lashed solidly down.

8 — If you have a crew, position them along the weather side of the boom and tell then not to let the gaff take them overboard. It's going to have a damn good try.

9 — The person in the cockpit should be ready with a lashing to catch a turn around the gaff and boom. This will be crucial to the survival of all hands.

10 — When everyone is standing by, wait for a 'smooth' in the seas, then ease the staysail quickly to leeward and sheet it in as hard as you can.

As soon as the hove-to equilibrium is broken, the boat will start to luff. She won't pass through the wind because she won't gather enough way, and the seas would stop her even if she did. Watch her luffing, feel her, and just as she is as far up to windward as she's going to go, let the halyards off. The sail will be on the shake, and will come down at the run. It never fails, but you must have everything ready.

11 — As soon as the gaff comes within reach, the first priority is to secure its outboard end. Easier said than done, but strength is given to those who need it.

12 — If the boom is not in a crutch, you can now lower both it and the gaff to the deck with peak halyards and topping lift. Do this quickly because the sail will be going crazy.

13 — Lash the boom down and jump on the sail. Give it the tightest stow you reasonably can.

14 — Note how the vessel is lying now she has no main. She may need a trysail to balance her, or she may surprise you by still maintaining her position with the wind and waves mostly forward of the beam.

15 — If you are content with how she lies, splice the mainbrace, set a watch, then turn in.

HELMING IN BIG SEAS

The windward performance of a light, short-keeled sailing craft is drastically affected by the skill of her helmsman. Every wave will stop her if it is allowed to. The only way to keep her moving is to luff a little towards each crest, then bear away over the top of the wave so that the yacht does not pound into the trough and slam herself to a standstill. If you do it right, famous progress can be achieved. Get it wrong, and even if all your teeth don't drop out, you'll make depressingly small gains.

The gaffer doesn't work like this. In all but the biggest waves she should be settled into her 'groove', so that her own momentum can carry her through. If the waves are steep enough to have become a serious consideration, she won't be pointing better than 55° or so to the seas by this time. This helps her not to slam, and she has so much displacement and power that for the most part the waves won't stop her, so long as she is sailed full. Try to point her up like a Bermudan sloop, though, and the only direction you'll go is sideways.

Downwind, she'll be much easier to steer than a short-keeled yacht. The unpleasant point of sailing for a traditional vessel is in a heavy beam sea. As she falls off the waves her displacement smacks her into the trough and buries her lee side-decks, even if you are not technically over-canvassed. The answer is to reduce sail still further. This will not only press you down less, it will also reduce your speed, which is almost always a winner in bad weather. If this fails to do the trick, and you can't stand the hammering any more, a comparatively minor course change sometimes serves to make life less alarming. When the strategic situation renders this unsafe, there is little choice but to heave-to.

Off the wind in hard going, a tiller-steered boat may become tough on the helm. You can make life a great deal easier by rigging a simple line around it. One end is tied off outboard, the bight is led round the tiller with a full turn if necessary, and you sit to windward holding the free end. The friction may not allow you to pull the tiller to windward with the rope, but it will certainly help you to hang on. The best way to steer is to pull the tiller itself a little further to windward than you need. Take up the slack, then ease the line steadily until the boat is going straight. After a few moments she'll begin to round up. Snatch another portion of weather helm and start the processs again. This technique works admirably aboard *Jolie Brise*. When the 38ft boom makes its presence felt, the only alternative is to stand on the deck and lean the small of your back against the tiller. That's okay if you are feeling energetic. For the aged pen-pusher, it's the tiller line every time.

A full relieving tackle each side of the tiller can be set up in extreme cases. In days gone by, this was standard equipment on large yachts, but now that there are few real racing craft surviving, such extravagances are mercifully rare.

SURVIVAL TACTICS IN THE OPEN SEA

Running off

This is a popular option, because it produces the results of both keeping the boat end-on to the seas and diminishing the apparent wind. A light vessel may find that she runs so fast that broaching becomes a real problem. The heavy-displacement boat needs a great deal of wind before she begins to worry about such matters.

The technique is extremely useful if the gale is going your way; because every survival mile you put in is another mile off your passage total. It is simply a matter of reducing canvas as the wind rises. At some stage you will have to drop your mainsail and that is the crux of the whole business. As we have seen, this is no sort of a party, but once it is done, a great sense of relief will pervade the ship.

In the end you may find you have to take every stitch off her and run under bare poles. I have done this in a 32-footer in force 10, and felt no need to go on to the next stage, which is to slow the boat down by streaming warps. By the time your affairs reach such a pass you may be concerned about the danger of being swept end to end by a breaking wave, or pooped. If this seems probable, you must choose between bearing it if it happens, or trying another survival option.

Running is apparently not ideal for every deep-draughted vessel however. The late Dr Pye, an ocean cruising pioneer, found that the deep forefoot and lean entry of his small west of England fishing vessel tended to make her dig her bows in. The problem must have been significant for so modest a commentator to mention it at all.

Heaving-to

Heaving-to is by far the most comfortable way of riding out a moderate gale. Unlike running off, it offers the bonus that no one need be permanently on deck. A well-found 30-footer will sit out a full force 8 in open water like this, while a larger craft will tolerate much greater wind strengths before her crew become concerned lest her rags of storm canvas blow clean out of the bolt-ropes.

A gaffer with a deep forefoot makes little leeway hove-to. Indeed, by juggling the headsail sheets and watching the slick of your drift, you can often arrange for the only movement to be directly across the wind. This phenomenon was of immeasurable value to working craft, and it can still save the ship when land is too close to leeward for comfort.

Sooner or later, however, any boat will find that there is too much wind around for her to carry any canvas at all. You will then be faced with the task of dropping the mainsail, and either running off under reefed staysail, or lying a'hull.

Lying A'hull

This method of storm survival has received considerable adverse publicity in recent years. This stems from the undeniable fact that for many light, beamy cruisers it is an extremely dangerous thing to do. Most sailing vessels left to their own devices end up more or less beam on to the wind. This means that they take the seas on the beam as well, and a glance at the stability analysis of many yachts is enough to show that in steep waves, this is a one-way ticket to capsize.

The traditional vessel has entirely different stability characteristics. It is the moving wave that knocks boats down, so capsize in practice is a matter of dynamics. Whilst it must be clearly understood that a big enough wave will invert any boat afloat, the heavy hull and spars of the gaffer produce tremendous inertial resistance to being rolled. The wind in the bare rigging maintains her at a safe angle of heel, and her long keel damps down any tendency to be wrenched in all directions by every lump of water which comes by.

Lying a'hull is not comfortable, but being at sea in storm force conditions is not the place for you if ease is your prime motivation in life. However, in a good gaffer, it is a realistic survival option. I've done it on two occasions for periods of over 24 hours in a 13 ton Colin Archer. She never once looked like being knocked over, even though we opted for the technique because carrying sail was out of the question.

Apart from the safety considerations, a short keel doesn't stop the boat going sideways at all well when it is not moving ahead. The long, deep keel works any time.

In a strong gale, an unattended production cruiser could easily be suffering 4 knots of leeway, while a pilot cutter making 1½ knots would be seriously bothered about her poor performance.

There is one word of warning about lying a'hull. In a big sea the helm should be lashed amidships. If it is fixed to leeward, when the boat is thrown into a downwind attitude by a sea so that she gathers way, she will round right up. If she does this up the face of a wave, then stops, she will be thrown backwards onto her rudder which may suffer damage as many tons of boat effectively land on top of it.

The Sea Anchor

A sea anchor is a large canvas cone, open at both ends and held in shape by a timber framework. It is streamed from the ship's bow or stern so that she rides to its drag, either facing the gale, or greeting it with her aft quarters. This unsuitable device was well publicised a hundred years ago by a Captain Voss, who made some remarkable voyages in a small sailing canoe. His book, *'The Venturesome Voyages of Capt. Voss'* makes clear that he owed his survival to the extensive use of the sea anchor.

It would be wrong to speak ill of the dead, and the troubles of Captain Voss's canoe were certainly mitigated by his methods, but the experience of many people since his time have indicated conclusively that the sea anchor is not the right thing for a heavy displacement craft. The strains on the anchor are horrific, the chafe is a constant enemy, and the whole boat is being forced to fight the approaching seas rather than give with the punches, which is her natural tendency. Deployment has frequently culminated in loss of the equipment, or damage of some kind to the boat.

Modern parachute-style sea anchors perform excellently for lightweight multihulls, and lifeboats tow drogues to keep their sterns up to the seas while crossing dangerous bars. In the past, yachts are on record as having achieved similar results in open water, but these have been isolated incidents. Recent research in the US has concluded that drogues be recommended for light displacement craft to tow in storm conditions. Try one if you think I may be wrong, but the current consensus seems to be that the system has no relevance for a gaffer.

Motor Sailing

The greatest single change in our circumstances from those of our forebears has come about through the arrival of the reliable auxiliary. If you find yourself having to work to windward in extreme conditions, nothing boosts the performance of any rig like a touch of the 'iron topsail'. There's no dishonour about motor-sailing. After all, we tow our propellers around the ocean. Uncomplaining, we suffer their dreadful drag and we tolerate the raising of our centres of gravity which the installation of an engine always entails. We may as well extract the benefit when we need it. So drop the staysail, sheet the main amidships, and the storm jib as hard as it'll go without ripping out the clew. Now select 'half ahead', and watch the lee shore disappear astern.

✪✪✪✪✪✪✪✪✪✪✪

Lone Wolf shows a fine spread of canvas and moves well in the lightest of airs.

CHAPTER XII

LIGHT WEATHER

Light conditions present their own special challenge to the gaff-rig sailor. Even in a modern gaffer, the ratio of working sail area to displacement is likely to be less than that of a Bermudan yacht with a masthead genoa or a balloon spinnaker. However, gaff rig offers unique possibilities to the creative crew for making good this deficit. In the calm waters generally selected by Old Gaffers' Race committees some amazing acreages of canvas can be spread, giving delight to the eye, and a vital extra knot or two downwind. At sea, unfortunately, some of these 'party frocks' cannot be worn for reasons of chafe and potential gear loss, but this question will be considered as it arises in the next two chapters.

The average gaff-rigged yacht of under 35ft ought to be able to carry all her working 'lowers' to windward in force 4. She may also manage her topsail, but if she can do so close-hauled in force 5, she is probably undercanvassed. Larger vessels, particularly ex-fishing craft, often show remarkable power to bear sail. In contrast, a modern cruiser-racer of 35ft will be popping in her first slab reef at the upper end of force 3. By the time it's blowing force 6 she's probably on her third reef and down to her number 3 headsail. She does, however, perform marvels in force 2 with main and No. 1 genoa. No gaffer I have ever dealt with is producing any performance to write home about in force 2, unless she is using her light-weather canvas. By today's standards, her displacement and wetted surface are just too great for her sail area. This is the penalty for her capabilities in a blow.

Happily for us, while it has been rightly said that you can't have everything in this life, by cramming on the big sails a gaffer can have a good try.

INCREASING THE POWER OF THE MAIN AND TOPSAIL

Unless you have a ringtail*, or a huge jackyard topsail made of lightweight cloth for such occasions, there isn't much you can do to increase the size of what is set abaft the mast. Nevertheless, there are one or two adjustments which can help these sails to give of their best.

The Mainsail

This can be made slightly fuller in light airs by easing the peak halyard a few inches. The sail should be hoisted, as usual, until the wrinkles appear between peak and tack. Then, unlike the normal hoist, the peak should be eased until they have just disappeared. Once you are sailing and the apparent wind builds up, you may discover that the peak looks too low, which will be evidenced by creases running from throat to clew. Even a hint of such wrinkles ought to turn the skipper's face ashen with shame. Tweak the peak purchase an inch or two until they disappear. For some reason, a flax sail is much more susceptible to this sort of adjustment than one cut from polyester.

The peak halyard purchase, if you have one, can be used as a fine tuning tool, just as a modern yacht might use halyard tension or a cunningham hole. Racing in a well-run craft in the sort of moderate breezes where there is a big difference in apparent wind speed on different legs of the course, the peak halyard is re-adjusted after each mark.

A loose-footed mainsail can be powered up considerably in its lower sections by easing the outhaul. Even if this causes a small amount of backwinding immediately abaft the mast, it usually is still worth the effort. Occasionally, the drive of a sail with a laced foot can be increased like this, but the effect is less dramatic.

In Chapter IX, we considered the vital element of twist in the main and topsail. In light airs, a certain amount of twist is especially desirable because of the greater differential in apparent wind bend. If you have a heavy boom, its weight will kill any twist at all when there is hardly enough air to fill the sail. Where this is happening, try topping up the boom slightly on the weather lift, watching the effect as you do so. It may help the gaff to fall away a short distance. Watch the luff of the topsail closely. If it is not lifting in the twisted state, it will certainly be generating more useful drive, because it is 'facing' further forward. Should topping up make no observable difference, scrap the idea. Perhaps it doesn't work on your boat, but at least giving it a try kept you busy for a while.

The Topsail

Even though there is only one line which has any real effect, a topsail can still be shaped up for light airs, particularly when it is set to leeward, and even more so if you are off the wind.

The magic rope here is the topsail sheet, which, significantly, is sometimes known as the outhaul. An outhaul affects the shape of a boomed sail. The sheet controls the angle it makes with the centre-line of the boat. In the case of a sail that has no boom, the sheet does both jobs. The topsail is unique in this respect: its angle of set is under the remote control of the mainsheet, while the topsail sheet usually outhauls it as hard as it will go, in order to keep the sail reasonably flat. In light airs, however, the sail can be given far more flow by easing its own sheet.

When the sail is to leeward it will swell out into a fine driving curve, often producing as much power as the rest of the rig put together, by virtue of its position in the

The topsail sheet here is just 'started' a few inches to power up the sail off the wind.

undisturbed airstream well aloft. When it is to windward of the peak halyards, only the top section will benefit from this treatment. Even so, it will respond favourably.

On the run the sail can be let off until it bellies almost like a spinnaker. Close to the wind you will need to be more circumspect. Once the boat is moving, and the apparent wind has built up somewhat, you may see the sail lifting at the luff, indicating a need to flatten it a little. Give the bight of the sheet a gentle pull, watching the sail all the while. If it helps, heave in a handful and belay. You'll be surprised at how hard it is pulling.

The Main and Topsail in rough water

A topsail can take some fierce punishment when there isn't enough wind to put it to sleep and the seas are throwing the boat around. Infuriatingly, this happens frequently at sea as any movement of the mainsail is magnified by the gaff. In the end, you start calculating the time the sail is actually setting and subtracting the amount of time it is inside out. If the answer is near zero, you may as well cut your losses and drop it. Don't capitulate, however, until you have done everything possible to quieten down the rig. A heavy boom will be less prone to kicking about than a lighter one, but when it does begin to snatch, every bang will go right through a caring soul.

In light airs, masts, booms and gaffs behave themselves close-hauled, except in extreme circumstances. The further off the wind you are steering, the worse things become. Luckily, as the boom is progressively squared away, it becomes ever easier to rig a preventer from its outboard end to the foredeck, just as you would when running dead downwind. In that case, the preventer is rigged as a safeguard against an involuntary gybe. Its purpose in light airs is to keep the boom from crashing around and dragging the sail, the gaff and the topsail with it.

To rig a preventer, bring the boom inboard and attach the line to its end. Now let the sheet off further than you will ultimately want it. Make the preventer up to a strong fitting on the foredeck (the bitts are often best, if the lead is good), and swig it as tight as you can. Come back aft and haul the mainsheet in against it. You should end up with the boom held rigidly. The whole job can be made easy by keeping a preventer permanently rigged under the boom. When it is required you have then only to lead it outside the shrouds and hook it to a dedicated tackle rigged on the foredeck. Sadly, not many boats have such a system.

As soon as the preventer is rigged, set up your gaff vang if you have one. There is nothing more to be done now, but often this will be enough.

The rig suffers most at times like this. Fittings are constantly wrenched around, while sails and ropes are chafed mercilessly. Being becalmed in still water can be a spiritual delight for a crew not pressed for time. In a seaway, it is one of the worst experiences the ocean has to offer. In many ways it is tougher than all but the harshest gale. As the wind drops and the damage increases, you will ultimately become more than happy to sacrifice the 1 or 2 knots you may still be making, in return for peace. Drop the headsails and topsail, then sheet the mainsail in hard amidships.

The chafe will cease, the main will help ease the rolling and you can go fishing, or inspect the level in the whisky bottle. You might even start the engine and trundle away in search of wind.

Looking back on my own experience so far, I have suffered far more damage to gaff rigs in calms than in storms.

HEADSAILS

This is the department where a gaffer can really pile on the sail. The foretriangle is usually anything up to double the length of that on an equivalent Bermudan yacht, and giving it its full share of attention will result in handsome dividends. As on all boats, working headsails should not be sheeted too tightly in light airs, but in the end, there is only so much that these small areas of canvas can do. It is the big stuff that delivers the difference.

The Balloon staysail

These can be carried in any wind in which working lowers would not be overpowered, but they are extremely useful in light airs. They are also known as Reaching Staysails because they do not usually set well close-hauled. Sailing trawlers called them Tow Foresails, because their extra power was invaluable when the trawl was being towed.

A balloon staysail is cut to the full hoist of the forestay, but it is a very much deeper sail than the working staysail. Its leech overlaps the mainsail like a racing yacht's genoa; indeed, the clew sometimes comes as far aft as the cockpit. The sail has a exciting tendency to lift a boat along rather than to bury her bows, possibly because it sheets so far aft. Its foot and leech are often of virtually equal lengths so that if you don't mark the tack clearly, you'll be forever in danger of hoisting it upside down.

Don't worry if the jib sheet girts across the
bunt of the balloon staysail. 'What can't be
cured must be endured', and the chafe
should be minimal, so long as both sails are
kept filling.

Nothing moves a boat in light
airs like a genoa.

Some boats contrive to set their balloon staysails when working to windward in light
going, sheeting the sail inside the shrouds. I have tried this on two different craft, both
cutters, and have had but little success, the mainsail being backwinded to such an
extent that the losses seemed to outweigh the gains. However, Dixon Kemp in his
Manual of Yacht and Boat Sailing (1884) states unambiguously that 'on a wind, the
sheet is generally brought inside the main rigging.' Furthermore, I have a photograph
of the great Royal cutter *Britannia* thus rigged, so who am I to say it doesn't work?
Obviously it does for some craft. I suspect, therefore, that success depends on the cut
of the sail. Working craft tow and reaching foresails are only rarely seen set inside the
shrouds. *Britannia*'s sail was cut very flat indeed.

The real power of a balloon staysail clicks in with the wind on or abaft the beam. A
big one is worth at least half a knot on most boats, and it will pull like the proverbial
Suffolk Punch. The sheet must be led well aft, and you may find that no satisfactory
lead exists. This can let the clew lift too high, allowing the upper part of the sail to
twist so much that it spills out its wind. This tendency can be cured by rigging a
downhaul onto the bight of the sheet. Ideally, this should take the form of a lizard,
which is a bullseye worked into the end of a lanyard. The sheet is passed through the
bullseye, with the lanyard being made fast to a cavil or a convenient chain plate. If you
don't want to bother with this gear on short reaches, you can make fast one end of a

short length of line, take the bight over the sheet, then haul down on the end. This will parbuckle* the sheet to whatever level you require. There will, however, be chafe between the two ropes if the system is left rigged for an extended period.

Giant Jibs

A full hoist jib, from bowsprit end to top-masthead, deeper in draught than a Yankee, is a winner for getting a boat moving. They were often known among English working boatmen as spinnakers, but technically, that is not what they are. Sometimes these sails are strongly made, and can be carried until sheer terror drives a crew to take them in. Others are gossamer thin, and will fill with air when no wind can be felt. A ghoster like this cannot live in more breeze than it takes to blow the steam away from the skipper's tea, but still it will be of tremendous value if you are not easily persuaded to motor.

There is no official way to rig a big jib. Some craft set them flying, some hank them on. Some send them out hooked onto the traveller, others shackle them to the cranse iron at the bowsprit end. Occasionally, in a boat which does not normally set a jib topsail, they are hoisted on the jib halyards, but they are more usually hauled aloft on the jib topsail halyard.

Achieving a reasonably straight luff can be a problem in all but the lightest airs, especially if the sail is hoisted on the jib topsail halyard, which is unlikely to have more purchase than 2:1. Clap a handy billy onto the fall if the luff won't straighten up. If that doesn't bring it into line, it is time to take the sail in, because something is bending somewhere. For all you know, whatever it is could be giving serious thought to the idea of springing or carrying away.

These sails are so powerful that they can do a deal of damage if left up too long, particularly if they are hoisted to the topmast, or tacked down to an unstayed bowsprit. Steady nerves are required to carry one in anything over 7 or 8 knots of breeze. Unless made of the lightest material they take up so much room when stowed that few cruising boats have one in their lockers. They are race-winners though, on any day when folks are scratching around for wind.

Mizzen Staysails

The mizzen staysail of a ketch or yawl is at its best at similar wind angles to a balloon foresail. It is hoisted to the mizzen masthead and tacked down on the weather side-deck, often on a strop, and often in way of the main running backstay chain plate. The sheet is usually led through a turning block on the mizzen boom and belayed near its goose neck.

If there is no purchase provided on the halyard, and something of a breeze is blowing, it will help to hoist a large sail in stops, then break it out with the sheet when it has been mastheaded. Whatever you do, though, don't forget to set up the mizzen running backstays before you hoist.

The mizzen staysail is the one trump which the yawl or ketch can play when confronted with the cutter's otherwise superior performance. It is a lovely sail, easy to manage, and a great puller. To own such a craft and not have one is a shame. In fact, the sail is so useful that for his solo circumnavigation, the late Sir Alec Rose actually removed the mizzen sail from his Bermudan yawl, *Lively Lady*, and left it at home, boom and all. He didn't reckon it was much use, and besides, it interfered with the mizzen staysail which he was ready to swear by.

Light Airs in schooners

There is almost no end to what a schooner's first mate can order up out of the depths of the sail locker when the wind drops below 10knots. He'll have a big jib, of course, and quite possibly a balloon staysail as well, but his great delight will be the gollywobbler. I have toyed with the idea of offering a definition of this special item, but have decided to back off, as I have seen so many variants. Its official function is to fill the gap between the two masts. The fact that the foresail is already doing this on a full gaff schooner doesn't seem to make any difference.

For what it is worth, the gollywobbler I sailed with was like a sort of giant fisherman staysail. It was set to leeward of the triatic stays which join the two mastheads, and to windward of the foresail. With the true wind abaft the beam we went so fast that we pulled the apparent wind forward until both foresail and gollywobbler drew at the same time. If you'd stood in the slot, the gale ripping through it would have torn your hat off. No one ever tried, though, we just used to hang on with stupid grins and hearts pressed up against back teeth, wondering who would chicken out first, the mate or the skipper. It was always the skipper because he had to front up the money for the sailmaker's bills.

The Rachel B Jackson *may look delicate ghosting through the islands of Maine, but she weathered an Atlantic storm which sank at least one larger vessel.*

CHAPTER XIII

DOWNWIND SAILING

STRATEGY

The essential difference between running and the other points of sailing is that when close-hauled or reaching, the sails are working as aerofoils. On a run they simply push the boat along.

The wind flows cleanly around an aerofoil, from luff to leech. On a running boat the angle of incidence between the wind and a sail prevents the air from flowing efficiently round the back. The airflow past an aerofoil is accelerated, particularly if there are two or more sails involved. This does not happen on a run, and the power of the wind is further reduced by the subtractive effect upon the apparent windspeed of the boat moving dead downwind.

All this makes for poor sailing performance. Add the ever-present risk of gybing and the unpleasantness of rolling along before a following sea, and you will see why running is a dead loss. It is to be avoided if remotely possible.

In all but strong winds, the only way to make any boat go well on a run is to hang up as much canvas as possible. This is easily done on a Bermudan yacht by setting a balloon spinnaker, which, with the latest in handling equipment, does not deserve its reputation as something of a 'bear'. Gaffers need all the sail they can spread, but this is not as conveniently come by, or as effective as a modern spinnaker. A great deal of muscle-flexing is required to set a big boat up for a run, and unless she is fully crewed, the job will not be popular.

The pain divide comes somewhere between 30ft and 40ft in length. Below this line, booming-out poles are readily handled and the sails can be humped around by one person. Above it, hard work awaits. It's great fun on a summer's afternoon in the Solent with four or five chums and a keg of beer on board. When the wind drops and hauls right aft halfway down the North Sea at night, the prospect is less pleasant.

Fortunately, on a long passage, it is often possible to avoid running at all. The best advice I ever had on the subject of passage planning was offered free of charge by an old delivery skipper. 'Don't try to steer down the rhumb line if it's not convenient,' he

Downwind, an imaginative gaffer can really pile on the canvas.

said. 'Always remember that the wind won't stay where it is for ever, unless you're crossing in the trades. Steer where the boat is comfortable. So long as you're going in the right general direction, you're in good shape. It'll all even out in the end.'

The substance of this pep talk is that one should stay on a broad reach rather than a run. You can always gybe and come in on the other tack if the breeze doesn't change. If you do you'll go faster, have a jollier time, and cover surprisingly little extra ground.

A 60-mile passage downwind might take 12 hours, rolling your stick out at 5 excruciating knots. If you were to come up 35° for the first half of the trip, then gybe through 70°, the motion would clean itself up and you'd certainly increase speed to 6 knots. The extra distance to sail would be 13 miles. If all things remained equal, you would arrive 10 minutes later, but in any case you would be fresh and happy.

Working downwind in a series of reaches

The boat which stands 35° out from the 'dead downwind' course will sail faster in all but the strongest winds, and she will always be more comfortable. In moderate airs she may well complete the passage as quickly as the boat which opts for the dead run.

When a run threatens, you should move heaven and earth to rant away on a broad reach with your balloon staysail singing in the wind. Any boat will be grateful, particularly if she is a ketch or a schooner. These craft reach superbly and are even less content on a run than a cutter or a sloop. This is because the schooner's mainsail or the ketch's mizzen blankets the sail in front of it, unless both are set goose-winged (one either side). This is okay in calm waters, but it can be extremely hard on the helmsman in a seaway.

There are times when a direct line to the destination is required whatever your vessel; then it is 'groan you may, but run you must.' In fact, if you are even 10° off a dead run you'll be far more comfortable, but your rig doesn't really start working until the headsails will draw properly on the same side of the boat as the main; so for our purposes, anything with the wind setting 20° or so from dead aft can be considered a run.

MAINSAILS ON THE RUN

Whatever else you do to make the boat go well downwind, the mainsail will still be the sail it has always been, stretched between gaff and boom, perhaps with a topsail set above it. On a run, the sheet will be eased right away so that the sail will tend to press up against the aft shrouds, and the topmast backstays. In calm water this is no cause for concern. The further out the boom can be allowed to swing, the easier will be the boat on the helm, provided that the gaff does not twist away forward of the thwartships line. If it does, its capacity for generating a roll needs to be experienced to be believed. Having ensured that the gaff is behaving itself, it doesn't matter if the boom is resting on the shrouds, unless you are a fetishist for varnish. So long as the sail is steady and not kicking around, it will do itself no damage by distorting its canvas against the rigging; the sail will only start to chafe when the canvas saws back and forth against the wire. In practice, this rarely happens even at sea, except in light going, so chafing gear to prevent damage from this cause is an unnecessary source of windage in most boats. The gaff may have a rough ride moving against the upper standing rigging, but this spar can be readily protected by screwing a couple of lengths of half-round brass strips to it in way of the chafe.

The Topsail

The sail which suffers most from chafe downwind is the poor old topsail, especially when set to leeward. As the gaff swings, it nips the sail between itself and anything that will take a bite out of it. One of these triangles of canvas can disintegrate in its lower portions over the space of a night. It requires watching with the utmost care, so that you might be forced to take it in just when you really need it. The only truly effective protection for a topsail is to stitch and/or stick a large sacrificial patch over the area subject to the greatest mincing action.

Use of a gaff vang, if you can manage to rig one, is the finest chafe preventer of all.

118

Watersails

The 'fun' way to increase downwind sail area is to set a watersail. These are draped under the main boom and receive their name for obvious reasons. Because they are so low down, they do not pull as hard as you might hope, but in races they have a shattering psychological effect on the opposition. To see a long-boomed gaffer overtaking from dead upwind with spinnaker (see page 117) on one side, and main, topsail and watersail on the other, is devastating. She seems to fill the sky, while the air for 50yds ahead of her is so still that the victim's pipe-smoke goes straight up as his yacht is inexorably overhauled.

The most desirable feature of a watersail is that it comes your way at the popular price. You already have one on board. It's called the working jib, or the storm jib, or whichever one happens to fill the gap. The tack is hauled out to the boom end, the head is hove up hard somewhere above the rail and the clew is sheeted aft to some convenient point of attachment. If the luff is too long, tie a knot in it. If it's too short, find a bigger sail, and if the clew is more than half an inch above the mean waterline, you can expect the bird from the rest of the fleet for being half-hearted.

The only problem with a watersail is that it renders the helmsman 100% blind. This leaves him little alternative but to pour himself a stiff gin and experiment with exchanging no vision for double vision. Never set one without posting a sober look-out of conservative judgement on the leeward side of the foredeck.

The problem with watersails is that the helmsman is totally blind on his lee bow. An extra look-out is the only answer.

STAYSAILS

With main, topsail and perhaps watersail pulling on one side of the boat, something is needed on the other to maintain balance, as well as provide extra sail area. If the run is going to be so short and there is no time to rig the spinnaker or balloon staysail, this is best achieved by booming out the working staysail with the whisker pole. You may also want to use this arrangement for running in heavy weather.

You can try goose-winging the sail without a pole, but it rarely works. The backdraught from the mainsail is so turbulent that the staysail refuses to settle down. The jib is even worse.

On a boat under 40ft, a working staysail can generally be boomed out with a whisker pole. This is a light spar whose length will be something like three-quarters of the boat's maximum beam. It should have a bayonet fitting on the outboard end to accept the bight of the sheet. Its inboard end fitting can be anything at all, including a simple rope strop, or snotter, that will give it full freedom of movement on the forward side of the mast. A whisker pole will stand more stably if it is rigged with a topping lift and a downhaul, although these can be casual affairs whose upper and lower ends may be rolling hitched to the shrouds, or tied off on a handy deck fitting. To rig a whisker pole, attach the lift and downhaul loosely, catch the bight of the weather sheet of the goose-winged sail in the bayonet fitting, then shove the pole outboard until the inboard end can be fitted to the mast.

As soon as the pole is rigged, make up its control lines and trim the sheet.

The larger the boat, the more unseamanlike the above procedure becomes, but the essence of a whisker pole is quick, easy operation, which requires no agonising about whether or not to employ its services. On a 30-footer or smaller, such a spar causes no problems. At 50ft or more, dancing around the foredeck, balancing a pole which is detached at its inboard end and attached to a live sheet at the other, can be nothing short of dangerous. In such craft, the staysail should be boomed out on a full spinnaker pole, properly rigged (see below), as would be the case in any boat running with the balloon staysail.

A poled-out balloon staysail offers an excellent compromise for skippers who do not wish to become involved with spinnakers, or sails set from the bowsprit end. A balloon, with its clew spread outboard and its belly as well flattened as possible, is a fine running sail which, if sensibly handled, will always remain controllable.

If you have a boomed working staysail of a generous proportion it is fruitful to come up with a system for helping it to set 'goose-winged'. This is sometimes achieved with great success, a conspicuous example being *Wylo II*, the Nick Skeates-designed cutter, in which he circumnavigated with no more sophisticated downwind gear than this. Booming out such a staysail is simplicity itself, and can solve a number of problems at the touch of the helm.

THE SPINNAKER POLE

All sorts of arrangements are seen today for controlling booming-out poles, but no one has come up with anything better or more straightforward than the old fashioned method. Although it was developed for use with the single-luff spinnaker (see page 122), this is still the most effective and the safest system for poling out a headsail of more than about 120sq ft. If everything is working for you, and you are fit and strong, you may be able to manage a whisker pole on a larger sail. However, there will never be any doubt about when the job starts to become hairy, and such a cobble-up just isn't worth going over the side for.

The great advantage of the spinnaker pole is that it is entirely self-supporting on its own lifts and guys. It is fully-rigged before the weight of the sail ever comes onto it, and so is as safe as can be.

The heel of the spinnaker pole is generally fitted onto some suitable goose neck at the mast, opposite the main boom goose-neck and attached to the same mast band. Its weight is supported by a topping lift rigged from a block above the hounds. In a small craft this will not need any purchase so it can be a 'straight up-and-down, one-each-side' arrangement. This is ideal because it facilitates hoisting the pole on either tack. If you need a purchase, a whip through a single stropped block on the fall will be adequate on all but the largest vessels. The topping lift is traditionally attached to the pole halfway along its length.

The hoisted pole's freedom to swing fore and aft is curtailed by a foreguy and a guy (or after-guy), attached to the outboard end of the pole. These are sometimes shackled to a cranse iron, but are often finished with handspliced eyes, and looped over the pole end.

The guy will need power, so if no winch is available it can be rigged with a purchase, tended from the after deck. In many cruising boats the most convenient way of arranging this is to use the weather staysail sheet purchase (or winch). This will be redundant while the spinnaker pole is deployed. The foreguy can often be handled without a purchase.

At the upper side of the outboard end of the pole is attached the outhaul block, through which the outhaul will be passed. If this line can be man-handled, the best place to make it fast is a cleat near the heel of the pole. If the sail is too powerful for 'Armstrong's Patent', it can be led through a turning block near the mast, and thence to a winch or a purchase.

Poling out a Staysail

The essential feature of this manoeuvre is that at no time does the foredeck crew become involved with the loaded sheets of a goose-winged sail. They are thus protected from one of the most dangerous devices created by man. The order of service proceeds like this:

1 — Close-haul the sail on the lee side of the mainsail. This will keep it quiet and safely out of the way.

2 — Rig the pole. If it is much longer than the foretriangle (as it was in the racing yachts of old), you'll have to loop on the guys before shoving it outboard. You should also lead the weather staysail sheet through the outhaul block and back inboard at this stage. Make sure that it passes over and forward of the topping lift.

3 — Supporting the weight of the pole on the topping lift, push it out until you can engage the inboard end in the goose-neck fitting.

4 — Allow the pole to settle comfortably forward of the thwartships line and hoist it to approximately the right height to set the sail.

5 — Make fast the guy, and take up the slack in the foreguy. If you don't, the pole may 'sky' when the pull of the sail comes on.

6 — Tell everyone to stand clear.

7 — Ease away on the lee sheet and haul the weather sheet (which is now officially designated the 'outhaul') so as to gybe the sail onto the boom.

8 — Belay the outhaul, then ease the foreguy while trimming the pole aft with the guy until the sail is set to your satisfaction.

To de-rig the pole, the opposite sequence is put into operation, bringing the sail across into the lee of the main and close-hauling it before anyone touches the pole itself.

Oversized balloon staysails and genoa jibs can be boomed out safely by this method. It may sound like a lot of effort, but once the pole has been rigged, handling it is a complete joy when compared with any other sort of attempt to achieve the same result.

THE SINGLE-LUFF SPINNAKER

Without doubt, the doyen of the downwind sails is the spinnaker. Some gaffers nowadays have removable outer forestays to enable them to use balloon spinnakers with contemporary sheet and guy systems. You can find out how to deal with these in any book on handling a racing yacht, but I note that some Old Gaffers' Race committees are frowning on such sails. It must be said that if pure performance and stacking up the silverware is your motivation, they are hard to beat, but my own feeling is that gaffer racing is not about winning at all costs. This question and various others along the same lines will be expanded in the last chapter of the book.

The spinnakers favoured at the height of racing gaff rig, as well as on early Bermudan yachts, including J-class giants, differed from those of today in that they

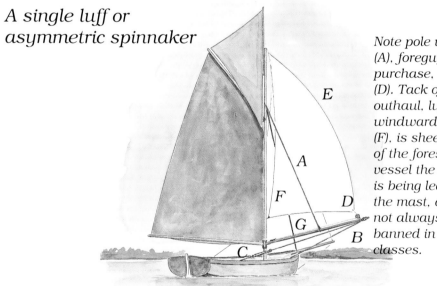

A single luff or asymmetric spinnaker

Note pole with topping lift, (A), foreguy, (B), guy with purchase, (C) and outhaul, (D). Tack of sail is fast to outhaul, luff, (E), runs to windward, while the leech, (F), is sheeted to windward of the forestay, (G). On this vessel the spinnaker sheet is being led to leeward of the mast, an arrangement not always favoured and banned in certain racing classes.

were asymmetrical. On a modern spinnaker the luff and leech are only differentiated by which edge of the sail happens to be on the windward side of the vessel, in the same way as they are on a squaresail. The asymmetric spinnaker has a luff and a leech, and never the twain shall alternate. It is a taller, narrower-shouldered sail than its current offspring, and is handled quite differently.

Hoisting the Spinnaker

Much grief can be avoided by stopping up the sail with rotten cotton or rubber bands. This is done by starting at the head, then working luff and leech through your hands, stopping the sail as you go, until you reach the foot. Leave the tack and clew clear of the bottom stop.

1 — Set up the spinnaker pole so that it is about 45° forward of athwartships and well topped-up. Take up the slack in the guy and foreguy.

2 — Shackle the halyard to the sail, making sure that the rope is passing on the correct side (windward) of the forestay. A swivel is a must between halyard and sail.

3 — Bend the outhaul onto the tack. This must pass outboard of the topping lift. Check also that it is led clear of the guys.

4 — Secure the sheet loosely to a suitable point on the lee side just abaft the mast, or bring it through a fairlead in a similar position. Some craft carry the spinnaker sheet further inboard than this, and on very small yachts I have seen it led to weather of the mast. Wherever it ends up however, the sheet must remain on the same side of the forestay as the rest of the gear.

5 — Hoist the sail as smartly as possible to the masthead.

6 — When the halyard is chock-a-block, haul away on the outhaul. The stops will probably begin breaking out before the tack reaches the boom end, but by this time they have done their job.

7 — If you have a struggle with the outhaul because the sail is now filling, ease the sheet until the luff lifts and try again.

8 — As soon as the tack is right out, square the pole by hauling the guy. You'll need to slack up on the foreguy, and this must be done carefully in a breeze, because it is the foreguy which is holding the pole down. Ease the sheet as far as you can during this manoeuvre.

9 — When the sail is up and drawing, trim the sheet in the same way as you would any other.

10 — It is perfectly in order to hoist the spinnaker without stopping it up, especially in light winds, but if you do, be careful not to outhaul the sail before it is mastheaded. If it fills prematurely it may go in the water, possibly with dire consequences.

11 — If the boom tends to 'sky' while running in a strong wind, try squaring the pole further and easing the sheet. If this doesn't work and the problem seems chronic, it can be addressed in the long term by moving the lead of the guy further forward. In a modern yacht, the spinnaker guys are led inboard at the so-called 'point of maximum beam', which is generally just abaft the mast. This makes a great deal of sense, and while the longer, old-fashioned spinnaker pole will not respond quite so well to this treatment, something of the kind will usually effect a satisfactory cure.

Dropping the spinnaker

1 — Top up the boom. Sometimes, the lift will have been eased so that the weight of the boom is on the sail. If this has happened and the pole is not topped up, it will fall into the sea when the outhaul is eased. This might be inconvenient, it will certainly be untidy, and it will be disastrous if the boat is moving fast.

2 — Ease the guy forward, taking up slack on the foreguy, then slack away the outhaul, man-handling the foot of the sail towards the mast while doing your best to spill the wind from it. Don't let go the sheet.

3 — When the sail has been hauled inboard from the boom, and not before, the halyards can be started, and the canvas bundled up on deck. In light winds, the sheet is let go and the whole sail gathered neatly as it comes down. Releasing the sheet in a breeze, however, is a formula for a lively few minutes.

Gybing an Asymmetric Spinnaker

There is no stock way of gybing a traditional spinnaker, and this is one of the main drawbacks of the sail when compared with its modern counterpart. A balloon spinnaker can, of course, be gybed repeatedly by a skilled crew without ever touching the halyard, or spilling a puff of wind. The only answer with the old single-luff variant is to drop it, shift the pole over, re-rig the gear, and start again. Nice work for a team of twenty paid hands in 1905. Not much fun for most of us. This doesn't detract from the usefulness of the sail on long legs, however. Some would say that sailing downwind in calm water without one was like a day without sunshine.

THE SQUARESAIL

For a long downwind passage in rough water, such as a trade wind crossing of an ocean, there is nothing to beat a squaresail, from all accounts. I have no personal experience of these in small vessels, but their advantages are obvious. A squaresail does away with the ever-present possibility of a gybe. It is easy to handle once it is set. It is virtually chafe-free if carefully thought out. It can be used with the wind anywhere from right aft to, perhaps, 60° on either quarter, and it generates excellent helm balance.

On the distaff side, one doesn't want the weight and windage of a yard and all its gear aloft when trying to work to windward. We have little to give away in upwind performance, and leaving a yard up the mast is tantamount to handing it out on a plate. The gear should therefore be readily raised, lowered and stowed.

Squaresails have been used with great success by many gaff sailors, but they have created a myriad of individual systems for handling them. Some are ingenious, some awkward, some might work on any suitable craft, others are exclusive. If you are planning the sort of voyage where a squaresail could make sense, you can do no better than scour the second-hand bookshops for the works of those yachtsmen of the thirties and fifties who specialised in converting working vessels into ocean cruisers.

For myself, I am content with a poled-out balloon staysail and a main set above a heavily-guyed boom.

TWIN HEADSAILS

For several decades in the mid-twentieth century people experimented with running under twin headsails. In many cases, particularly in Bermudan craft with tall masts, this was highly successful. It offered excellent steering characteristics in the days before the invention of the true wind-vane self-steering gear. It was reasonably flexible concerning wind direction, and it had the overriding benefit of cutting out chafe completely.

I rigged my first ocean cruising gaff cutter with 'twin' headsails for trade wind work, but I must confess that the results were disappointing. Basically the problem was twofold. The boat rolled far more than was her wont, and she went inordinately slowly unless the wind was at least force 5. The system certainly gave our wind-vane steering mechanism an easy ride, but we scrapped it after a few days, rehoisted the main, and never looked back.

Our running sails were of a respectable size. One was our balloon staysail, the other was an impressive reacher sold to me for £7 by a friend, yet they did not have enough area between them to compensate for the loss of the mainsail. Nonetheless, a number of gaff-rigged small craft were apparently successfully rigged with twins in days of yore. Dr Pye set them on his famous *Moonraker*, and his book *'Red Mainsail'* gives photographs of another small vessel plying down the trades under a tiny pair of staysails. She seems to be making a fair lick.

The only advice I can offer if you are tempted to give twins a try, is to do what I did. We invested little money in the system initially. Had it worked out to our satisfaction, we would probably have rationalised it. Since it did not, it cost nothing to re-employ all the gear elsewhere on board. The only item that seemed for a while to be superfluous was the second booming-out pole, but even that found a useful function during the tropical summer as a spreader for a full deck awning. Very shady it was, too.

✿✿✿✿✿✿✿✿✿

CHAPTER XIV

SLOW-SPEED SAILING

The plain fact is that most gaffers are nowhere near as easy to manoeuvre as their Bermudan counterparts. Jinking around amongst the moorings in a short-keeled, lightweight yacht with a powerful headsail is child's play to any competent sailor. That so few owners of such craft demonstrate any willingness to sail them into tight waters reflects more on them than the vessels under their command.

To handle any gaffer demands skill of a far higher order, but this does not mean that we should all start the auxiliary as soon as the pier-head is in sight. On the contrary, the satisfaction increases in proportion with the difficulties. It would be a mistake, however, to imagine that nothing has changed since men of old sailed everywhere in the days before the internal combustion engine was invented.

The world was a very different place in 1890. A fisherman approaching harbour had no decision to make about whether or not to use his engine, because he didn't have one, he'd never had one, and he'd never been on a boat that did. His whole thought process was instinctively at variance with our own. Even those of us who have chosen boats without engines have spent much of our seatime in craft which, at the touch of the starter button, will perform the impossible. They will drive straight up into the eye of the wind, and continue to move until we put them out of gear. If we so choose, they will stop long before their way would be naturally lost, by dragging it off with the propeller thrashing in reverse.

The essential variation in our view from that of the nineteenth century seaman is that we can always decide we don't like the look of things, and motor. Pre-Motorboat Man had no choice. He either worked his vessel into her berth by non-mechanical means, or he went somewhere else.

This didn't automatically make all our predecessors into perfect boat handlers. When you examine old photographs of Scottish harbours, full literally to the brim with unwieldy herring luggers, you realise that jamming all those boats into so tiny a space must have resulted in many a broken bowsprit, and splintered bulwark. Nonetheless, the tactical appreciation of how a boat was placed in relation to her destination and

126

the wind direction must have been finely developed in such men. It is that appreciation, coupled with a deep-seated understanding of what a particular boat will and will not do, that is the essence of any boat handling under sail.

Slowing down and stopping are at the core of most manoeuvres, and it is in these that the greatest differences exist between the gaff-rigged craft and the modern yacht. The principles are the same, the techniques often vary.

When no tidal stream is running and there is no shortage of turning space, one would normally opt to lose way with the wind forward of the beam. If the tide is running to windward, however, or the boat must be slotted into a narrow gap before stopping, a down-wind approach may be required. The techniques for losing way in these two situations are entirely different, so it is essential to decide from the outset which is to be employed.

To put it at its simplest, if the final leg of an exercise can be carried out with the wind well forward of the beam it will be possible to spill wind from all the sails and so control boat speed. If, for reasons of tide or space, the wind is on or abaft the beam, any attempts to dump wind from the mainsail (and any other boomed sail set abaft a mast) will be in vain. It will therefore be impossible to lose all way unless radical steps are taken.

On entering waters where space is limited, you will often wish to reduce speed long before this crucial decision needs to be taken. Losing way while retaining full control of the boat is one area in which the gaffer is more able than the modern yacht.

There are two reasons for this. The first is that because it has more sails, and a bowsprit, gaff enjoys a greater degree of flexibility than Bermudan. Secondly, since most gaffers have a deep forefoot and a long keel, their resistance to being pushed sideways holds up until they are virtually stationary. This is often not the case with a fin-keeler whose forefoot is cut right back. As she slows down her keel stalls easily and her head 'blows off'. This happens to gaffers too, but they are far more forgiving. They are also slower on the helm, which is just what you want at sea, but it doesn't do a lot for the cause when you are sailing in amongst the moorings. You should therefore always be thinking in advance of your next turn — two tacks ahead for river sailing, for example, instead of the one which generally suffices for small Bermudan yachts.

GENERAL METHODS OF LOSING WAY

Headsails

Assuming you have taken the obvious step of lowering your topsail(s), shortening down the foretriangle is often more effective in slowing the boat than the comparatively small reduction in area would lead you to believe. Headsails do not only drive in their own right, they are also improving the efficiency of the mainsail, so that any reduction in their work output is of double value.

Since most gaffers won't sail at all well under mainsail alone, this means of controlling speed is not open to the sloop. Any vessel rigged with a cutter foretriangle, however, can do herself a great deal of good by stowing her staysail on entering an anchorage. The gap between jib and main is then so large that it generates no appreciable slot effect, and the rig is depowered considerably as a result. Little is lost in manoeuvrability, however, because the jib's leverage from the end of the bowsprit is tremendous. It counteracts the fact that a gaff main carries its area further aft than the Bermudan. This does not alter as the sail is reefed, which is one of the reasons why a gaff sloop or cutter points up so high when she is hove-to.

If you have a Wykeham Martin jib furling gear, as many small and moderate-sized craft do, sailing in with your jib set on its own up forward is doubly satisfactory because when you've picked up your buoy, or come alongside, or anchored, it can be rolled away at the heave of a line.

Most boats will be seriously unbalanced without a jib, unless the main is well reefed, or the mizzen has been stowed. Taking in the jib will certainly diminish your way — possibly more than the staysail — but you will pay dearly for the privilege, losing the edge from your steering just when you want it most.

A further advantage of sailing in without a staysail is that, large or small, the foredeck is clear for the crew to handle ground tackle, moorings or warps, while the helmsman or a crewman stands by the jib sheets aft. Even if the jib sheets belay forward as they do on certain large craft, having the working area clear of the sometimes dangerous and always inconvenient presence of the staysail, is a popular move with crews.

Mainsails

If you have a ketch, yawl, or schooner, much can be achieved by dropping one boomed sail. The question of which one can only really be answered by individual experiment, though many ketches balance sweetly enough under headsails and mizzen. A yawl, on the other hand, may find herself in a state of gutlessness without her mainsail.

Schooners, as in most things, enjoy the best of all worlds. Being so far aft, the main produces maximum luffing effect, yet by dropping the foresail, it is robbed of the slot that brings it to life. Even so, some schooners are happy to pirouette under foresail and headsail with the main stowed in the crutch. The way to find out is to try your boat with every possible combination of sails, long before you ask her to go yachting through the eye of a needle.

Sloops and cutters enjoy none of these advantages. If the wind is forward of the beam they can always spill some of it, but if they are to slow down with the wind abaft the beam, they must destroy the drive of that big square of canvas. This can be at least partially achieved without dropping the sail, either by oversheeting, or by scandalising.

Oversheeting

This works by spoiling the airflow around the sail. To function properly, a sail must cut the airstream cleanly, developing lift by bending the wind without interfering with its smooth progress. If it is undersheeted with the wind forward of the beam, it stops driving, because the air blows equally down both sides of it. By oversheeting grossly, the airstream is allowed to create a huge eddy on the lee side, stalling the sail. The only drive it produces in this state is push from its own windage. As an aerofoil it has ceased to exist.

Don't expect great things from oversheeting, but it might knock your speed down by up to 35%. Its only drawback is that it plays havoc with the balance of the boat by increasing weather helm, sometimes to alarming degrees in gusty weather. If you are likely to want full power back in a hurry, though, it's a winner. It only takes a couple of seconds to ease the sheet.

Scandalising

If you have a loose-footed main attached to the mast on hoops, you can depower it almost 100% by this means, reducing its windage conclusively at the same time.

1 — Top up. Use the weather topping lift if there is a choice.

2 — Let go the tack downhaul and overhaul its purchase.

3 — Trice up the tack as far as you can, using the tricing line.

4 — See if this is a sufficient reduction of area. If not:

5 — Ease away on the peak halyard, letting the gaff drop below the horizontal. There is now virtually no sail left setting.

6 — If you need a small amount of canvas for a few moments it will be easier to let down the tack than to peak up, with all but the smallest sails.

Tricing

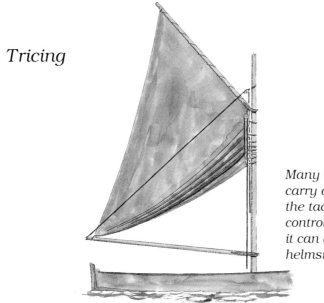

Many loose-footed mainsails carry a tricing line to haul the tack aloft. This not only controls sail area quickly, it can also improve the helmsman's view forward.

Cachalot trices up her tack to slow down and keep station with the Dunkirk Little Ships' fleet.

7 — Where the tack is permanently attached to the boom, the power of the sail can be reduced by over 50% by simply letting off the peak. Before doing this, check the arrangement at the gaff jaws. A well-designed fitting will keep the throat halyard and the throat of the sail in a vertical line, parallel to the mast, no matter what angle the gaff is making. Often, particularly with gaff jaws or saddles made recently, this feature is lacking. The effect usually is that as the gaff begins to droop, the throat halyard attachment point moves outboard. This produces a fulcrum, from which the long lever of the gaff wrenches brutally upwards on the luff of the sail. I have seen the throat pulled out of a main as a result of this design fault. If you are stuck with so misbegotten a gaff saddle, always start the throat halyard a foot or two before easing the peak. That gives it enough slack to survive the dreadful leverage.

Spilling wind

The high-aspect-ratio rig on a current production cruiser is a wonder of controlability when slowing down and stopping on a close reach. On this point of sailing the skipper can juggle his speed to a nicety by spilling wind. When the speed falls too low, he can pull on a little mainsheet and, if necessary, some jib as well, to keep her driving gently. In this way a yacht can be maintained right on the edge of a stall without losing control, until she is luffed to a standstill at her mooring buoy, or alongside the quay.

Theoretically, a gaffer will manage this equally well. With a vessel up to about 30ft, it works perfectly in practice. Above this length the sheer physical nuisance of pulling in or letting out the sheet tends to militate against a smooth result. Blocks fall over so that the rope won't run properly. If there isn't much breeze the friction hangs things up, then one part of the purchase throws a bight around another and you can't pull it in until someone has untangled it. I used to cope with it on a cutter with a 21ft main boom, but the job was often awkward. With a 30ft spar it isn't a realistic proposition, unless you have two crew standing by the sheet and a third ready to push the boom out if required.

On a bigger boat, if you are wanting to lose way preparatory to stopping altogether, and have managed to organise a wholesome, close-reaching approach, you should steer towards a point well downwind of your final objective. Let the mainsheet run in good time. When you are dead to leeward, luff, and let her carry her way up to the mooring.

Carrying Way

No one can teach how far a given vessel will carry her way once the power of the sails has come off. If your boat will perform the close-reaching trick described above, you'll manage most of the time without ever really needing to know. If you have to luff your way off, you must make a judgement about this with almost every close manoeuvre you enter. A boat behaves differently in different conditions of wind and sea, and the state of her bottom paint is critical. There is no easy method for discovering the answer. You must find some quiet corner, and practise until you are sure.

Steering with sails

Because traditional craft generally have sweet, easy lines they are rarely ill-mannered under sail. Many a modern sloop will flatly refuse to bear away in a strong breeze until her crew lets off the mainsheet, especially if she is steeply heeled. Despite the centre of effort of the mainsail being located so far aft, a gaffer will usually turn away from the wind with the main pinned in, so long as she is moving well through the water. That does not mean, however, that she won't spin a great deal faster if you let the mainsheet off. The effect may not be dramatic, but in a tight corner it can make the difference between an expensive collision and a safe arrival.

Similarly, if you are tacking from a reaching course, pulling in the main as you luff up will assist the helm, making sure you don't miss stays. When you need to luff in a hurry and the boat is hardly moving, push the helm down, heave in the main and dump the headsail sheets. It may just help her make up her mind.

If you have lost way head-to-wind before you were ready, backing the headsail quickly will guarantee you fall onto the tack you want. It might be necessary to grab the staysail clew and physically hold it out to windward, because the message to the boat will then be far more positive than if it is merely weathered with the sheet. Don't forget to watch the water immediately over the side if you have to back the headsail. As soon as the boat begins to make a sternboard, reverse the helm to help steer her round.

Sternboarding

Some people think that this is the province of the 'boy racer' and his half-ton flyer, but I have done it regularly in the trade wind anchorages of the West Indies in a 30-ton cutter. A vessel which is sailing gently astern under full control will dig in her anchor as positively as though she were under power.

When the boat has lost her way head-to-wind, you have two choices, depending upon her personal habits. Some vessels, notably schooners and yawls, will drop back accurately, steering carefully astern, with the main or mizzen pulled in hard amidships like the tail of a weathercock. This is great if it happens. Most craft, however, need more persuasion.

Wait until you've lost way, then push (or pull with a rope) the main boom as far out to windward as it will go. The boat will begin to move astern. As she does, she will try to screw round in order to feather the sail. Do what you can to kill this tendency with the rudder, and push the boom out even further until the helmsman reports that she is steering.

Man-handling the boom can be something of an effort, but as you pour yourself a Cuba Libre, secure in the knowledge that the hook is firmly in the sand, it'll have been worth all the sweat.

✿✿✿✿✿✿✿✿

CHAPTER XV

PRACTICAL MANOEUVRING

The four classic set-pieces of all boat handling are mooring, anchoring, coming alongside, and the man overboard recovery. Of these, anchoring is the easiest, because it doesn't require the yacht to be stopped with pin-point accuracy. Anyone can anchor under sail in the most unwieldy vessel afloat, so if you've tended to play safe and motor in harbours, anchoring is a good project to begin a sailing career.

One of the first jobs undertaken as a square rigger came onto soundings after an ocean voyage was to make ready the ground tackle. In the days of sail, no small vessel would have entered harbour without an anchor available to be let go immediately, even if anchoring was not her prime objective. Auxiliaries have become so reliable that we have tended to become cavalier about this requirement, but if you are manoeuvring under sail with the bottom within reach, the anchor may still be a life-saver. It must therefore always be rigged for instant action.

Every boat handling exercise except man overboard depends on a correct assessment of wind, tidal stream, and the relationship between the two. Man overboard recovery is independent of tide, because both boat and man are being set in the same direction at the same speed. If anyone were to doubt this proposition, it can be illustrated by a game of snooker being played in an aircraft cruising smoothly at 500 knots. The balls would roll across the baize, undisturbed by the fact that the whole shooting match was plunging through the air at something approaching the speed of sound.

An escape route is a must when you are manoeuvring under sail. However perfect your scheme may be, the wind always has the last word, so you should always be sure to have an escape route ready. Unlike a boat under power, the sailing vessel reaches a point of no return, at which she must commit herself irrevocably to a course of action. At that moment, you have two options: either successfully complete the exercise, or bale out in good time. One or the other. No half-measure will save you, unless you have decided to leave your engine ticking over, 'just in case'. Even then, things can still get out of hand, so always leave room to abort. If the space just isn't there, you should think at least twice before trying the job at all, especially if your boat displaces more than four or five tons.

Velsia scandalises her main as she falls back to her anchor.

MOORING

Although it is easier to anchor a traditional vessel than to pick up a mooring, we'll look at mooring first because the process is simpler to describe.

No tidal stream

Shorten sail if necessary (Chapter XIV) to bring the boat under slow-speed control. Approach from the downwind sector with mainsail (or mizzen) and headsail set. Eyeball a spot a few yards dead downwind of the buoy. Exactly how far to leeward this should be depends on how your boat carries her way, but in force 4 and flat water, it could be a boat's length for a small, light vessel, or anything up to twenty or thirty yards for an unstoppable long-keeler. If you can't control speed before luffing the last of your way off, you may have to allow a greater distance still. I've known yachts carry their way for 100 yards and more. By this time though, you're on pure judgement.

Ideally, begin your final approach from at least 200 yds away. If this isn't possible, you'll have to be rather sharper in your actions. The heading for the magic spot should be a close reach. In a gaffer, this will be about 60° from the wind. If you are pointing higher than this, it will be difficult to lose way without the boat losing her grip and sliding into the dinghy sailor's 'no-go zone'. If you are so far across the wind that the boom ends up on the aft shroud, you'll never slow down at all.

The close reach for boat control

Boat A is too far to windward of her destination and cannot spill wind from her mainsail. Boat C is too far to leeward and cannot fetch her destination without tacking. Boat B is approaching correctly. She can spill wind at will, but still maintain control of her way.

Sail up to your designated point, checking your speed by spilling wind. By the time you are downwind of the buoy, you should be going so gently that you have almost, but not quite, lost steerage way. Now, luff the boat head-to-wind and pick up the mooring as she stops. The helmsman should try not to place the buoy under the bows. The crew's job is easier if it ends up somewhere between the stem and the shrouds. So long as it is forward of the pivot point of the boat, she will drop back sweetly as it is being brought aboard.

Lower the jib the moment the buoy is fast. The main can come down when you are ready.

If you have a bobstay, the helmsman should decide which side of it the buoy will pass, and keep the crew informed. On the final luff-up, the buoy may be out of sight from aft, so the boat-hook brigade should indicate its whereabouts. If they have prepared a slip-rope, and the buoy is on the wrong side, they may find themselves struggling. On a big boat with a high bow, it's a good plan for some young athlete to crouch down on the bobstay, ready to pass the slip-rope while the deck crew steady the buoy with the boat-hook. At all times the gang up forward should communicate with the 'driver'.

Wind with Tide

The only difference between this and the no-tide situation is that you will be set 'down' from your selected spot on your final approach. If the tide is very strong you may decide to abandon your 'luffing leg' in favour of carrying the close reach right up to the buoy. There is much to be said for this, but, if you opt for it, you should make sure that boat speed is only fractionally greater than that of the tide. This is because, after you have picked up the buoy, your boat will still be carrying her way. If she goes past it and you try to make fast, either you'll miss the mooring and have to start again, or she'll snub round beam on to the tide, the main will fill, and you'll have a messy kerfuffle while everything settles down.

Once again, the buoy is best placed on the shoulder of the boat as you come up to it. This makes it easy to grab. If it gets mixed up with the bobstay, you can't blame the foredeck crew for missing it. As soon as the buoy is alongside, luff head to tide, so that the relative positions of boat and buoy remain the same. This makes securing it a lightweight task. If the bow goes even partly across a strong tide, there will be terrible heavings and gruntings from forward, because your deep forefoot will take hold of the passing water, and start to sail away sideways far more positively than a fin-keeler ever would.

One final point. Any tidal manoeuvring can only succeed by the constant use of transits to define straight lines. If you are approaching a buoy across the tide, line it up with something, and keep it there. Then you'll always arrive. Similarly, if you spot something which you're concerned you might hit, see if it is moving relative to its background. If it is, you're in good shape. If not, alter course quickly, or reach for your fenders.

Picking up a mooring

Mooring when wind and tide are together, or at slack water. Boat approaching buoy under main and jib, spilling wind as necessary to control speed.

Mooring under sail with wind against or across tide. The mainsail is stowed; the boat approaches downwind under jib (or staysail) only, checking her way relative to the tide.

Wind across or against the tide

The crucial thing here is that your approach to the buoy must be up-tide. In circumstances where you can lay a course with your mainsail spilling wind, you will be able to work up to the buoy under perfect control. If the main won't spill, nothing you can do will slow you down. Yet if you were to come to the buoy in a down-tide direction in order to spill the main, the stream wouldn't allow you to stop. The only solution, if you are in any doubt, is to get rid of the main. You can then approach up-tide but down-wind, with a headsail alone to drive you. Wind can be spilled from a headsail whatever point of sailing you are on, so you have plenty of control as you creep up to the buoy. If your windage is pushing you over the tide even with the sail fully flapping, drop it, and proceed under bare poles. You'll have to be sharp grabbing the buoy as it goes by, but at least there will be no half-controlled canvas to aggravate your problems.

This is where, on the face of things, the gaffer misses out in relation to the Bermudan yacht. All currently produced three-cornered rigs will sail under headsail, after a fashion, even to windward. Any such yacht that has the remotest pretensions to class will tack under headsail only. Somewhere, there may be gaffers capable of this, but if so, they have kept their secret well guarded. This means that if you are to commit yourself to an approach under headsail, it will be inconvenient if it doesn't succeed first time. The point at which you drop the main must therefore be substantially upwind of your destination. On the other hand, if you overdo it, it may take you hours to work back against the tide, under your comparatively small headsails.

There are two solutions to this dilemma. One is superb judgement. The other is the scandalised mainsail. The latter is the ideal answer, especially if the sail is loose-footed and can trice up its tack. After the peak is down, you can produce, or dump, the area of up to half the sail with the tack downhaul and tricing line. On a smart rig, you can literally play them like the throttle of an engine. It's beautiful to watch, highly gratifying to perform, and the Bermudan sloop has no real response to it.

Getting under way

The same criteria apply to leaving a mooring as to picking it up. If the main will fill while it is being hoisted, you'll have to sail away under headsails. The main must be dealt with later, unless you can contrive to wrestle it up in a scandalised state.

ANCHORING

To anyone brought up on today's yachts, anchoring in a traditional, gaff-rigged craft is going to be a pleasant surprise. In the first place, the inertia of the heavier hull will encourage her to lie quietly to her cable. This is exaggerated by the deep forefoot and long-keel configuration. The boat simply does not want to be blown about by the gusts of wind sweeping through the anchorage. Her displacement also encourages her to carry sizeable ground tackle, rather than paring down this vital gear to the minimum size that could be safe under ideal conditions. Finally, in the case of the cutter or the yawl, the fact that the mast is set well back in the boat discourages the bow from surging in the gusts. The schooner's foremast often catches the wind, so in this respect, her crew enjoy less security than they might desire, but chunky cable and a good depth of keel can offer reasonable compensation.

Another benefit of gaff rig for cruising from anchorage to anchorage, is the bobstay. On many craft, it is possible to heave up the anchor until it hooks firmly under the chain. It can be carried like this for short passages in water that is not too rough, thus entirely doing away with the trouble and dirt associated with handling it. When the time arrives for it to be brought aboard, a heavy anchor can be easily lifted by hooking it onto the staysail halyard. One person can then hoist it, while another bears it off from the ship's side. If the anchor is a 'fisherman' type, it should have a lifting lug welded to the shank at the balance point.

The process of coming to anchor is much the same as picking up a mooring, except

Here the author's cutter appears to be committing the cardinal sin of sailing with her lee topping lift tight. In fact, she was about to tack and anchor. The lift is set up so as to be ready in good time. (Photo Jack Somer)

that, as we have noted, you don't have to stop the boat quite so accurately. If you are anchoring head-to-wind, wait until the boat is stationary, then let go the anchor and drop the jib if possible. Try to sternboard away (Chapter XIV) if you can. If the boat insists on falling off the wind, even with the jib down, do your best to make sure the main doesn't fill, because, if it does, it will probably make a nonsense of your efforts. I used to sail a gaffer whose forefoot was cut away so that she couldn't keep her head up. I usually ended up by dropping all her sails just before I let go the anchor, so that her own weight would dig the hook in as she fell back. This approach couldn't be recommended in a crowded anchorage, but it worked excellently in spacious surroundings.

If the wind is contrary to the tide so that you have approached your anchoring spot downwind under headsail only, douse the sail after dropping the pick, so that the boat can drift back with the tide. You could try letting fly the sheet, but even the windage of the flogging sail may prove sufficient to maintain way.

Is it holding? The late Connaught, *a Galway Hooker dating from the mid nineteenth century, comes to anchor with her jib down, but still hauled out to the bowsprit end and ready for instant use.*

MAN OVERBOARD

Every boat should have some sort of a system organised for man overboard, because when this emergency happens, action must be taken immediately. In a small gaff-rigged yacht, the classic method of reaching away, then tacking and returning on a close reach (as for the tideless mooring pick-up), may often be successful. This will not always serve in a larger craft. Here, it may be preferable to heave-to straight away by throwing the boat through the wind and leaving the headsail sheets fast. The boat will frequently end up to windward of the casualty, and if a line cannot be thrown far enough, drift can probably be controlled to bring her within heaving-line range.

Another method is to launch the dinghy. This can be done successfully from a 50ft cutter in any but the heaviest seas, so long as she is hove-to and the boat launched amidships to leeward. I have done it, and it works. It was standard practice for Bristol Channel Pilots a hundred years ago.

If you have a reliable engine and a vessel which can get rid of her headsails easily, you may find that the best approach is made from leeward under power with mainsail pinned in hard and headsails stowed. If you opt for this, always be aware of the danger of a rope being drawn into the propeller. In the heat of the action, it happens all too readily, especially on a traditional boat which has so much cordage. Make a drill of looking around the deck for stray lines before starting the motor, then look once more before engaging the gears. Finally, if you are picking up under power and sail like this, never forget that the propeller is a dangerous eater of limbs, and that your approach must be planned accordingly.

COMING ALONGSIDE

The process of sailing alongside a berth is sometimes no more difficult than picking up a mooring. It is also the most satisfying piece of work available to any seaman, and because of a traditional craft's capacity to carry her way, a well-mannered, heavy vessel can often execute it with more dignity than a skittish, short-keeled yacht. Most of us fight shy of it nonetheless, because the intimate presence of a hard dock and the probable proximity of expensive yachts psyche us out.

The first rule is to rig plenty of fenders and maintain a 'stopping rope' ready for instant use. This will be made fast aboard somewhere abaft the boat's pivot point, so that if the boat fails to fade to a standstill at exactly the desired spot, a crew member can step off with it, take a turn on the bollard, and surge* off the last of her way.

There are three different basic scenarios for sailing alongside:

Onshore winds

If you refer back to the section in this chapter about stopping on a mooring buoy, you'll realise that, regardless of the relationship of wind and tide, you will never be wanting to sail alongside with your mainsail set and the wind abaft the beam. Sometimes the wind will be onshore, and the tide will be non-existent, or running in such a direction that keeping the main up and spilling will be desirable. If this is the case, look carefully at where you are going. A gaffer's boom is long, and it can get into all sorts of mischief as it sweeps a pontoon, carrying all before it. Once again, the capacity to fully scandalise the sail solves the problem, if you can do it. Oversheet the boom and juggle the amount of sail drawing by using the tack downhaul.

If your main is permanently tacked down to the boom, this option may be less attractive. You'll therefore have to consider the possibility of coming alongside under headsail only, unless you are on a schooner. Schooner foresail booms are usually short enough to stay out of trouble. Fortunately, if the breeze is onshore, you won't be trying to drive the boat up to windward so you'll usually be able to sail in under headsail only. The job won't be as easy as it would in a yacht with a big genoa, but you should manage it successfully, even if it isn't always as elegant as you'd like.

Offshore winds

With the breeze forward of the beam as you approach the dock, you'll need your mainsail up to drive the boat to weather. If you are heading up to the tide it is often possible to make a neat close-reaching approach. First, pick up a transit ashore, next to the point where you want your cockpit to end up. Play your sheets until the transit is stationary while you are sailing parallel to the dock. You are now stemming the tide. Put the helm over gently and let the boat slide sideways into her berth. Nip ashore with a couple of ropes, then drop the mainsail. As with all these operations, it pays to have the topping lift set up ready, and the halyards coiled or flaked clear to run in good time. Who knows, you may want your sails down in a hurry. If you do, it's ten to one someone will forget the topping lift.

If the tide is running against the wind, but the wind is more offshore than on, you have the gaffer's joy. Stow the main and mizzen, then sail in under staysail or jib, spilling wind so as to be travelling at only a fraction of a knot more than the tide. Docking under sail in this way is every bit as safe as berthing under power. After all, the staysail sheet must be more reliable than the multiple cogs and bolts of a marine gearbox.

The Dead Loss

Every now and again, you'll come across a berth that cannot be entered under sail with the wind or tide as it is. In terms of boat handling under sail, the only thing that has really changed in the last hundred years is how people think. Every ancient commercial harbour has its walls lined with derelict capstans and warping posts. These were for use at just such times. Now, in our auxiliary-powered paradise, we are relieved of such labours. We hit the button, and drive in.

It isn't always so easy, though. Sometimes our engines are defunct, or you may favour that pure delight, a boat without power. If you are then confronted by a 'dead loss' which you nevertheless must enter, you are down to warping in from a berth close by (on the other side of the dock, perhaps), into which you can safely sail. You might be able to anchor off the berth, row ashore with a rope, and warp in, easing out cable as you go. If you don't want to launch the punt, you can always heave a line to a

A Grand Banks fishing schooner noses into a crowded harbour in the fog, manoeuvring under sail and anchor alone.

well-wisher, or float one ashore on a fender if the wind favours you. There is usually a loafer on the wall to make it fast.

If you've anchored off, let go more cable as soon as you're safely alongside, so that the whole length lies unobtrusively on the harbour bottom. When you are ready to leave, you are, as they say, 'quids in'. Bring your lines aboard, then haul off with your anchor. Hoist sail, break out the hook, and sail away in the finest traditions of the working seafarer.

Back in the 1960s, my first juvenile command was a 24ft gaff sloop which had no engine. My friend and I sailed her everywhere. It never crossed our minds that there was any other way. Much later, I made a two-year cruise with my wife in a 13-tonner whose engine gave up the ghost early on in the proceedings. Fixing dead diesels was not part of our voyage plan and was entirely outside our budget, so we went for a sail instead. They were the most carefree years of our lives.

HANDLING LONG-KEELED CRAFT UNDER POWER

This is a book about sailing. However, since most of our boats are equipped with auxiliaries, a few words on dealing with this important department of our lives cannot go amiss.

Compared with sailing, handling a boat under power is a push-over, but the sort of hulls which are generally placed beneath a gaff rig require more understanding than a yacht with a fin keel, a spade rudder like a barn door, and a comparatively powerful engine.

Many gaffers, particularly the older ones, are relatively underpowered. Some have off-set propellers, others flatly refuse to steer astern; they all carry their way to an extent that is positively exciting, and the majority throw their sterns like dodgem cars when the gearbox is put into reverse. They also feature bowsprits.

The question of carrying way is easily solved by manoeuvring at the slowest speed possible at which steerage can be maintained. This is a problem for a boat whose only serious draught is in the fin keel. A long-keeled vessel will be stable at slow speeds, even in a stiff cross-wind, because the bow grips the water and is not constantly trying to 'blow off'.

Prop-walk, or the sideways thrust of a propeller going astern, is a serious factor in handling any long-keeled vessel. There is nothing that can stop it happening, so you can only learn to live with it by knowing exactly what the boat wants to do. When this has been established, you can order all your turns and your comings alongside so as to pander to the vessel's preferences. In other words, never ask her to do something she won't like. If you do, and she refuses, you cannot blame her for the outcome.

You can establish which way a strange boat will kick by putting the engine astern while tied to a dock. Note which side has more prop-wash boiling up. In a free-floating situation, she will throw her stern away from the turbulence when the engine goes into reverse. This is dramatically so in the case of a vessel with an offset propeller.

When pure sailing craft were first being converted into auxiliaries, boatyards were unwilling to pierce stern-posts for the shafts. Neither did they wish to interfere with excellent steering characteristics by carving great apertures in perfectly shaped rudders. Instead, they usually opted for poking the stern gear out under the quarter, often on the port side. Those of us who own such craft are only too aware that putting a three-bladed propeller right into the boat's run is as good a way of slowing her down as towing a bucket. We compromise with our shame because, for coastal cruising, the knot or so which the screw costs us in light going is more than compensated for by the delight of motoring merrily up rivers against the tide, or into impossible berths.

The propwalk from an offset propeller is a marvel to behold. Whichever handed the screw may be, all its wash blasts straight past the deadwood and is shot out on the same side. It can't get out anywhere else because the keel is blocking its exit.

If your propeller is on the port side, therefore, the boat will tuck her stern in beautifully if you take way off with the engine while coming 'starboard side to'. Try going astern as your port side approaches the dock, and chaos is the only possible result. Short turns by putting the engine alternately ahead or astern are to be executed solely 'with' the propeller. This means the stern must be swinging to starboard and the whole boat turning to port. If you attempt to turn her 'against' it, in the unfavoured direction, she'll tell you exactly where you get off.

Even boats with a centre propeller behave like this to a certain extent. I skippered a Brixham Trawler which would turn in little more than her own length by going ahead and astern, never gathering way, with the rudder hard over the whole time. She had a big, 3-bladed prop firmly in the rudder aperture, and a keel as long as a railway carriage. She, incidentally had a more conventional propwalk. Her stern cartwheeled to port with the engine in reverse.

I have little consolation to offer if your boat won't steer astern under power. The only plan for improving your lot is to be constantly aware of the dictates of your propeller, and of how these may relate to any cross-winds. If the prop makes the stern walk to port, and the wind is going to blow the bow to starboard, the situation is beyond repair. You must therefore organise your manoeuvre accordingly. If, on the other hand, the wind were on the starboard bow, it might neatly counteract the propwalk.

Some boats are prepared to steer astern after they have reached a certain speed. With such a vessel you are at least in with a chance. So long as you have the space to gain control before swiping the neighbours with your bowsprit, all is well. If you know the stern will go to port until the critical amount of way has been built up, can you contrive to throw it to starboard before you start? If you are 'backing out' from a berth, you can sometimes arrange this by judicious spring-line handling, or, if the vessel is light enough, by giving her stern a shove. By the time she's reached steering velocity, she will be more or less going in the right direction.

The most important message is that, unlike sails, whose effects are almost infinitely variable, a motor can only drive ahead or astern. The complications caused by the propeller and the boat's windage are always foreseeable. If you consider your boat unpredictable, think again. She's talking to you. It's possible that either you aren't listening or that there's something about her accent you can't quite pick up. Accept her foibles graciously, and she'll do wonders for you. Fight them, even unwittingly, and you'll lose every time.

Bowsprits

Living with a bowsprit can come as a shock to those who didn't grow up with them. Bowsprits have an evil reputation. They are known by such rude names as 'prodder,' 'docking probe', and others which are not printable. People panic when they see bowsprits approaching their pristine yachts. One of the funniest sights I ever beheld was a lady ambitiously waving a collapsible plastic boat-hook in the direction of a 15ft example on the end of 30tons of straight-stemmed cutter. She needn't have worried. The boat was coming in with the propwalk, but I suppose she wasn't to know that.

The fact is that we don't hit other boats any more often with our bowsprits than they do with their own pulpits. It's just that if we are unfortunate enough to poke somebody, it's bound to be the bowsprit that does it, so these noble spars have an almost 100% strike rate. Thus are legends born. There is also the more sinister aspect to bowsprits about which Dr Freud, had he ever been asked, would have had much to say. However, this is a family book, so we will leave the father of psychiatry out of our deliberations.

A bowsprit is merely another part of the boat. Our noble vessels begin at the cranse iron, just as a modern yacht starts at her pulpit. The difference is that there is a large space underneath the spar before you arrive at the stem, so it is possible, and indeed usual, to sweep the timber across a pontoon in the critical stages of coming alongside. This can be a spectacular event, but it must be executed if the boat is to end up neatly parked. Failure to perform this frightener results in stopping some yards out, and you will then require the ignominy of a pull in.

Don't lose your nerve. Make sure you aren't going to pick up any fuel pumps, café tables, or 2CVs, then go for it. Even the great Maine schooner skippers have collected tree branches and other unwanted gifts, including a table d'hote menu and a clean napkin jammed in the cranse. None of us is perfect, but to be timid is worse.

To misquote from the Military, 'Who dares, gets alongside.'

✿✿✿✿✿✿✿✿✿

146

CHAPTER XVI

THE QUESTION OF AUTHENTICITY

When I first went to sea back in the middle sixties, all gaff-rigged craft still operational were there simply because they happened to have survived. There was no particular interest in them, and there was no talk of ever building any more.

Against this background, the materials with which the vast majority were fitted out depended on nothing more sophisticated than the depth of their owners' pockets. If you were dealing with one that had limped through since before World War II, always on a shoestring budget, you were probably going to be faced with an ancient suit of cotton sails. Very likely some of her halyards would be of hemp or manilla, while her blocks were all of the wooden-cheeked variety. On the other hand, the fortunate vessel whose owners had spent money on her, would certainly have had sails of polyester (Terylene™ or Dacron™) cloth. All her cordage would be of man-made fibre, and she probably sported a number of tufnel blocks.

At that time, there was less talk of restoration, and more of keeping things going. An 'old gaffer' was, frankly, a cheap method of getting on the water, and while many of us chose such vessels at least partly from preference, our perspective of their historic and personal value was very different from today's viewpoint. It was glaringly obvious, even then, that modern sails and ropes made far more sense than the old ones in nearly every way, so people started using them to replace worn-out traditional gear as soon as their price came within reach. Thought was rarely given to such questions as 'faithfulness to the original', or 'historical authenticity'. For most of us, those were not our motives for owning the boats.

In the sixties and early seventies, gaffers excited little comment merely for being what they were. To rig them with new materials which seemed better than the old was the most natural thing in the world. The same went for paints, varnishes and everything else, although enlightenment was beginning to glimmer over such major issues as converting a gaffer to Bermudan rig. This had been going on ever since the 1920s. Indeed, the old King's *Britannia* was one of the first to be so served, but by the second half of the century the practice was already frowned upon.

By 1980, the scene had changed. Enthusiasts were buying up early Bermudan conversions and restoring them to the original intentions of their designers. Replica craft were being built in modern materials such as GRP, and gaff rig had established a new place in the market. Regattas for traditional craft were becoming so popular that by the second half of the decade the great Breton sea festivals were attracting up to a thousand boats, and a quarter of a million fee-paying spectators. The circle is at last unbroken, and the question any of us with an interest in traditional craft, whether old or new, must ask is, 'To what extent will a voyage down the searoad to the past assist me and my boat as we sail into tomorrow's sunrise?'

I used to become involved in fierce discussions over this, just as I did over whether gaff rig was better than Bermudan for ocean cruising. Now, however, a modest amount of wisdom has displaced some of my youthful fire and I recognise that argument over materials and methods is utterly barren. The decision is, and will ever remain, entirely personal. It will probably, but not certainly, depend upon the sort of sailing you do, the amount of time you can make available for your boat, what your motivations are for owning such an anachronism, and who your friends are. Ultimately, it may be decided by your sense of smell.

Who could offer guidance over such diverse questions? Not I. Only you can know what will suit your crew, your boat and yourself. However, a policy is an excellent thing. It is far better to have defined your stance than to swirl along, governed by neither wind nor tide, a prey to whim at every fit-out. A boat whose owner is clear about how traditional she is will be faster, safer, and substantially easier on the eye.

Over the years I have been shipmates with most of the available alternatives for fitting a boat out. I have reached my private conclusions about what is best for me at the present time, but in different circumstances I know that my position would change.

For what they are worth, here are one or two thoughts on the subject.

SAILCLOTH

Cotton

When the New York Yacht Club schooner *America* wiped the floor with the Royal Yacht Squadron around the Isle of Wight in 1852, one of the secrets of her success was cotton sails. At that stage, the Brits were still yachting on the linen flax canvas preferred by all working craft from crabbers up to first rate men-of-war. The *America*'s cotton duck was more stable in shape. It was also lighter, and on these counts alone it beat the British cloth hollow.

It wasn't long before cotton was the favourite of all the yachting fleets, and so it remained until it was eclipsed in its season by the arrival of Terylene and Dacron.

Excellent though it was, cotton was not without disadvantages. It was not quite so strong as flax, nor as resistant to rot and mildew. Neither was it so long-lived. It 'set a treat', however, as a study of the superbly cut sails depicted in early yachting photographs shows.

Most cotton sails you are likely to meet today will be hanging on into old age as best they can. I saw a new suit cut in the middle eighties, but it was unique in my experience. Very beautiful it was, though, and its fresh, creamy smell was a delight to the senses.

Flax

At the time of writing, it is still possible to buy best Arbroath flax (Royal Navy issue) by the bolt within the UK, so long as you know where to find it. Perhaps it is this availability that has made the material popular with owners of traditional craft, until recently. If you want to be genuinely faithful to your boat's past, flax is the way to go if she was a working vessel, or, if she is modern, has the aura of one.

Tanned flax is the most beautiful material for making sails, if you can live with the problems it brings.

Because of its less than perfect shape stability, sails of flax were generally cut from a heavier grade of cloth than their cotton equivalents. However, the material lasted far longer than its racier counterpart and was ultimately stronger. Fishing boats used it exclusively, as did all traders and merchant vessels. The only commercial exceptions were occasional high-flying pilot cutters, but even those stuck rigidly to flax during the winter months.

While inshore yachts favoured cotton, ocean cruisers usually plumped for flax. Trysails and storm jibs were invariably heavy flax, roped all round.

For a gaffer operating today with the temptations of the new cloths staring her in the face, the benefits of flax are these:

+ Flax is longlasting. If it is looked after, a flax mainsail will last 10 seasons.

+ It is well-mannered. It doesn't chatter and flap hysterically while tacking in a strong breeze.

+ It is a joy to handle when it is dry, so long as you can cope with the weight. Stowing a flax main on the boom is a pleasure because, unlike Terylene, it doesn't try to slip off while you are passing your sail ties.

+ Flax is unaffected by the ultraviolet (UV) element in sunlight which ultimately destroys most modern fibres. This is generally beneficial, but it is particularly so if you intend to go on extended cruises in the tropics. Sunshine is good for the stuff.

+ A flax sail is easily repaired by hand without a sewing machine. Sail needles, palm, beeswax, spare canvas and plenty of linen thread are all you need. Cringles are usually worked onto the outside of a traditional sail, so they too are readily replaced at sea with no special equipment.

+ Because stitching beds into flax, rather than standing proud as it does with modern cloths, the natural-fibre sail is extremely resistant to chafe damage, most of which occurs at the seams.

+ Flax, especially when it has been tanned, (see Appendix 1) looks lovely.

It isn't all pleasure, however. Flax has its drawbacks, like anything else. Here are some of them:

— Nowadays, a flax sail will cost you more than one made in modern cloth. This is partly because of the amount of handwork that is unavoidable, and partly because of the rising cost of the material.

— You should never stow a flax sail wet when it is going to remain rolled away for more than a day or two. If you do, it will begin to rot. This means it must always be covered when left on the boom, and the cover must work one hundred percent. I permanently weakened a sail by employing an inefficient cover. This also means that if the sail is wet when you stow it, you have a problem. Once or twice, and just for a week or two, you'll get away with it, but life isn't like that. Without the utmost vigilance, it will happen time and again. If you must leave the sail wet, it seems best not to cover it. Then at least the air can blow round it, which is better than nothing. This wetness factor makes flax headsails a real labour of love.

— Even when dry, a flax sail is heavy, which means harder work in a short-handed craft. When it is soaking wet, the mainsail on a 32ft cutter is going to be all that two healthy adults can manage.

— The tanning comes off natural fibre sails onto your clothes. If you care, this is a drawback. The answer is to wear a canvas sailing smock, and take it off as soon as you've stowed your sails, otherwise you look like a 'salty sailor' around the town. No real yacht hand or commercial seaman would have been seen dead stepping out in a strange port without his 'going ashore rig' bent on.

— A new flax sail requires stretching in. This is an extremely skilled and specialised task. Do it incorrectly, and the sail will never be any good. Getting it right will take some time. If your sailmaker fails to make the correct allowance in his measuring of your spars, the sail will never fit properly either.

— Despite the best efforts of the sailmaker, a flax sail flattens off tremendously when it becomes saturated. It may even be pulled temporarily out of shape by the differential stretch between the canvas and the hemp bolt-ropes.

— Tying the reef-points of a wet flax sail can be tough, especially if it is the deep reef on a big sail. I have seen strong men totter below with their hands bleeding after tackling the job. It would have been easy by comparison with a polyester sailcloth.

— No full indictment of flax sailcloth would be complete without a word about its suitability as a source of dietary fibre to the rodent population. Traditional sails stored on the ground, or on shelves, are constantly at risk from being the main course of the Rat family's Christmas dinner. They've tried Terylene, and somehow, the flavour isn't quite the same.......

Synthetic flax

If you fancy the look of flax, but you can't cope with the problems, Duradon™, or something similar, may attract you if you have a cruising boat. Like everything else, though, it is not all gain. On the positive side, these products have the following advantages:

+ Looks like, smells like, tastes like the real thing (except to the discerning Mr and Mrs Rat).

+ It is strong and long-lasting.

+ It is cheaper than the real thing.

+ It doesn't absorb water to the same extent, so doesn't have such serious weight problems.

+ Synthetic flax handles well.

+ Its stitching is moderately chafe resilient, but it is not so good as flax in this respect.

+ It doesn't rot, so you can stow it wet any time you like.

+ It can be readily hand-stitched.

+ There are few stretching-in problems, so it is easy to measure for a new sail.

If all of this sounds a pretty seductive package, bear in mind the following:

— If you're going for authenticity, synthetic flax is not real.

— Since Terylene or Dacron, which are not real either, undoubtedly make a more efficient sail, you might feel that the material is deselected on this count alone. If appearance is of greater importance for your purposes than pure sailing performance, this may be irrelevant.

— It degrades to a certain extent in sunlight, though not so rapidly as other man-made fibre sail-cloths.

— Like tanned flax, it is not colour-fast.

— It does not hold its shape notably well. Indeed, some people say it is worse than flax in this respect.

Polyester Sail-cloths

These materials, under the brand names of Terylene and Dacron, ousted all natural fibres in a handful of years when they arrived on the scene in the 1950s. When you look at the advantages listed below, you'll see why. Since then, the cloths have improved beyond all recognition, so that, for short-distance sailing, it would be difficult to justify using anything else on purely logical grounds. Notwithstanding this, there is still much to be said in favour of flax for ocean crossings, and prolonged spells in the tropics.

However, if we were logical creatures we probably wouldn't be sailing the boats we do, so there may legitimately be more reasons for choosing a sail-cloth than pure expediency. The argument that we should have Terylene/Dacron sails, because if that cloth had been available in the 1890s everyone would have used it, is flawed. If engines had been around, they'd have used them as well. They did. As soon as they could lay hands on the machinery, all working seamen cut down their rigs and enjoyed the new freedom of going where and when they wanted. With a few anomalous exceptions, there isn't a pilot boat, a fisherman, or a trader in the developed world today who uses sails in any form. That shows us what the professionals thought of sail. To speculate about what they might have used had it been available is entirely irrelevant to our own situation.

Having sunk that quaint idea without trace, let's take an unemotional look at polyester sail-cloth. Here are its main advantages:

+ It is about half the weight of natural fibre.

+ It is far stronger, weight for weight, which means that your sails can be thinner, easier to handle, and even lighter. This is good for the crew and since your boat (if she is an old one) was created to bear more weight of sails up the mast, it will increase her power to carry canvas in a breeze.

+ It is impervious to damp and all its nasty effects.

+ It is colour-fast.

+ It requires only the most minimal stretching in.

+ Compared with traditional sail-cloths, Terylene and Dacron are wonderfully stable. Their shape will remain as it was built for years. Any boat should therefore sail better with a suit made from these cloths.

+ Tying reef points is not a feat of strength in a polyester sail.

+ Polyester sails are far lighter to hoist than those made in other materials.

+ So long as they are protected against prolonged sunlight by stowing in bags, or under covers, polyester sails last for years. Some modern cloths feature a certain amount of UV protection, which can only help with this.

Even polyester isn't all winnings. Here are a few areas in which it may be found wanting:
— UV degradation.
— Seriously prone to chafe on long passages. The stitching stands proud, and sits there waiting for sheets or shrouds to wear it away.
— A polyester sail is not 'user friendly'. Working on it is an unpleasant affair for the amateur, and your results are liable to be less satisfactory than in natural fibre canvasses.
— Stowing a 'plastic' sail is not much fun either. It is pleasantly light, but it slips about all over the place. At sea this can be a particular problem.
— Polyester sails are fussy and noisy.
— They look horrid (when compared with flax or Duradon) when they are stowed. No one notices the difference when they are set, except at the closest of ranges. They only see the lovely curve of a sail which has not blown out of shape.
To revert to the oldest cliché of the lot, 'you pays your money(sic) and you takes your choice'.

CORDAGE

After a suit of flax sails, nothing perfects the look of a traditional vessel like natural fibre rope for her running rigging. The trouble is, after the appearance and the smell have been written off, the only other thing to be said in favour of old fashioned cordage is that it is a joy to splice. In every other department, it is dreadful stuff. Fortunately for all but the purist (and thank heaven there still are some), it is now nigh-on impossible to find good quality Italian hemp. This was definitely the best rope for most marine uses. If it was unavailable, or unaffordable, the mariner would opt for manilla. As a last resort, sisal might be pressed into temporary service, but it really was temporary, because it never lasted any length of time.

I once served a six-month sentence aboard a 90ton ketch, which we rigged from the deck up with manilla. I was full of enthusiasm at the outset, but my optimism soon waned on a variety of fronts. The food was lousy, of course, but when it came to the cordage, after three months intermittently at sea between a wintry English Channel and the North Atlantic trade wind belt, the situation became akin to that down in the mine, 'Where the danger is double and the pleasures are few'.

Traditional ropes needed constant renewal, because they lost strength and rotted, rapidly becoming unreliable. They chafed easily and were extremely weak when compared with even the humblest man-made fibre. Many of them were rough to handle, and all suffered from shrinkage in the wet, so that halyards, downhauls, and particularly mainsail outhauls and peak lashings, needed attention if sails were not to be stretched out of shape. As well as this, wet rope jammed in sheaves unless blocks were oversized, and they were unwilling to render smoothly when forming a tackle.

And woe betide the hapless optimist who used a locking hitch with one on a rainy day.

Altogether, traditional ropes present a dismal picture to those of us unused to their lively characters.

At the lower end of the size scale, lacings are infinitely less trouble in man-made fibre small stuff, and for the same reasons. I suppose the devotee of the genuine article would point out that most seamen's knots were designed to be made in hemp and manilla, and that in these materials they never shake undone or slip out. This is undeniably true, but on the other hand, if you want to undo a manilla double sheet bend on a dark, wet night, you'll need a spare set of fingernails and a useful marline spike.

The situation with modern rope versus natural fibre is more clear-cut than with sail-cloths. Both main groups of sail fabrics have much to be said in their favour. The only people who would use traditional cordage today are those running their boats as authentic floating museum pieces. There is nothing wrong with that. Indeed, I have every admiration for them, but for people who are clocking up high mileages with their yachts, natural fibre cordage is hard to live with.

The only exception to this is good old tarred marline. This is sold in every chandlery in the land. I suspect this is because its evocative smell misleads the public into believing they have entered a salty world of real buccaneers. Every gaffer should use this for her servings, even if the two-strand black nylon fishing twine, from proper chandleries in down-town seaports, is stronger, rot-proof, chafe resistant, and lasts for ever. We are romantics at heart, after all. Let us allow ourselves at least that much indulgence.

If marline is regularly maintained by painting it with black varnish twice a year, it will go on for ever. It will also keep water out of handsplices far better than any nylon, because it squidges together so beautifully as you crank it tight with the seizing mallet. When you have ladled on extra tar (see Appendix 1) or the black varnish, no water can get through if the serving is really doing its job. It smells great, too.

GENERAL BOAT ALTERATIONS

All of us have to decide about sail cloth and cordage, but if you have a new boat, that could be the sum of your agonising, particularly if she is not a specific replica. Those of us with older vessels have an endless string of minor decisions to make.

Do we rip out the electric light and return to oil? Do we remove the staysail sheet horse someone installed in the l930s? Should we continue to tolerate that fascinating original petrol engine, when a new diesel would be half the size, twice as powerful, and ten times as safe? In my own case, do I rip out the excellent wheel steering conversion, now 40 successful years old, and replace the original tiller with a reconstructed substitute?

The answers to all these are, as we have noted, subjectively decided. However,

Gaffers — even old ones — make great ocean cruisers.

unless you are actively setting out to be the curator of a perfect reconstruction of the past, each question should be tackled by a further query.

'Is the early modification I am thinking of doing away with, making my life any easier?' Presumably it did for the person who originally installed it. If it has made the boat genuinely better for her current purpose, and it isn't a gross eyesore, why not leave it?

Similarly, if you are deeply worried about the petrol engine, take it out, or sell the boat. The fact that you are thinking seriously about it as a responsible owner, means that in your heart the decision is already made. The only thing stopping you is an honest concern not to spoil the boat's authenticity. The fact of the matter is, you don't want the boat to be original, because you and everyone else knows that even 1930's petrol engines are extremely dangerous. Having worked through the problem so far, if you still can't bear to do the job, your only recourse is to find a different boat that is less explosive, and let your successor blow himself up instead.

It's odds-on that the first thing the new owner will do when your back is turned is to change the engine anyway, and once it's done, does it really matter who did it?

The same test could be applied to the enlargement of working boat rigs, or the cutting down of yachts. It's you who must live with the boat you have, but there is a degree of responsibility to the integrity of the ship, and to generations yet unborn. If your alterations diverge too far from the original, perhaps you should seriously consider changing your vessel instead.

The use of modern balloon spinnakers in gaffers' races does not transgress the great issues in any way. It just makes me feel rather sad. Little is proved by winning and losing at these events. A racing yacht of the nineteenth century, against a fishing smack of 1885, with a Breton lugger thrown in for variety, is a rich recipe for a grand day's spectacle on the water. The interest lies in watching the various boats perform, and in trying to get the best from your own. It does not, or should not, lie in winning at all costs. Remember that if fishermen could have used balloon spinnakers, they wouldn't have bothered, because these realists were well under power by the time they had been invented. Races should show how the boat sailed in her heyday, not the performance increase which can be brought about by application of the owner's bank roll.

If this is what pleases people, I don't criticise them personally, because one can have lots of fun hanging up outrageous sails. It does, however, seem to detract from an event, and to cast the spotlight onto the immortal observation of Grantland Rice:

> .... when the Great Scorer comes
> To write against your name
> He marks — not that you won or lost —
> But how you played the game

One action which I firmly believe history will find unacceptable, is to make major changes of an irreversible nature to a classic vessel, which so far has escaped significant modification. If you are really worried about that petrol engine, lay it up carefully, store it in the garage, and make sure that your new diesel fits the original bearers. You can do no more. What is unforgivable is to buy a gentleman's yacht, which may be the only surviving example of her type still innocent of tampering after 80 years, then start sawing off deck beams and burning the old cockpit sides, so you can have a bigger 'sitting area' for Sunday afternoon picnics with a crowd of business chums.

Don't laugh. It's been done, and I think the only way to end this chapter is with another quote. This one is from Dickens' Sam Weller:

> 'It's over, and can't be helped, and that's one consolation, as they always says in Turkey ven they cuts the wrong man's head off.'

The mizzen topsail picks up the last of the sun aboard a Brixham trawler.

APPENDIX I

LOOSE ENDS

The one thing a well-run ship should never have is loose ends. They are an offence to the eye, and may turn out to be dangerous. However, as I have written this book, a number of items have cropped up for which no home offered itself. They need a mention nonetheless, so they are all tucked into this ditty box. Some will be irrelevant to what you are doing, but perhaps the odd one will be of assistance.

STOCKHOLM TAR

If you are using marline for your servings and soft seizings, it will need freshening up once or twice a year with Stockholm Tar. There is no real substitute for this soft-scented product, and I am pleased to announce that it is still readily available from Scandinavian chandlers. Due to the rising power of the conspiracy to reduce all things to mediocrity, it has become exceedingly hard to come by elsewhere.

Stockholm Tar is made from a distillate extracted from the roots of pine trees, which differentiates it from all forms of coal tar. It seems that ladies and gentlemen of the agricultural and equine persuasions make use of Stockholm Tar on the hooves of their beasts. It can therefore be acquired from horse chandlers, and very good their version is, too. It doesn't quite have the magical aroma of the essential Viking product, but, faute de mieux, it will do well enough.

The main problem attached to tarring your rigging is that, depending on the weather, it will remain sticky for days afterwards. This often upsets the guests. The only answer is to be circumspect about when you do the job, or to favour black varnish as a realistic alternative.

BLACK VARNISH

This bituminous unction is sold in cans. It smells like road tar, and creates a fine finish over all seizings and servings. It sinks, after a fashion, into 'bare' yarns, but its main function is to form a thick, shiny, impervious skin which will waterproof the whole job. The over-riding advantage of black varnish over Stockholm tar is that it goes off in an hour or two. The best policy for seizing maintenance is to carry the two products on board, and make sensible use of both.

LANOLIN

One of the delights of gaff rig is that it generally employs galvanised gear. This is cheaper to buy than stainless. It is not so strong, weight for weight, but you employ bigger shackles to compensate, which are far easier to handle with cold, wet fingers.

Another benefit of the galvanised shackle is that its threads are less finely engineered. After it has been spannered up it will be unwilling to unscrew itself, so it isn't necessary to wire every shackle on board as you would with stainless steel. Generally speaking, only shackles aloft require wiring, unless they are crucial to the survival of the rig (forestays, for example). In this case, being doubly sure never goes amiss.

A galvanised shackle, or any other galvanised thread, will seize through rust formation if it is left wound up tightly for a long period. This problem can be solved by greasing every thread on board. By far the best grease for this purpose is old-fashioned lanolin, if you can still find any. Nothing better has been produced.

Keep a small pot of lanolin handy near the cockpit. If you don't, you'll get tired of going to the fo'c'sle twice a day and after a while you'll stop bothering.

MATERIALS FOR STANDING RIGGING

Stainless steel wire rope needs virtually no attention. This makes everybody love it, until one day it lets go unexpectedly. You are given no warning of any sort. If you are stuck with this unsuitable product, consult the manufacturers, and enquire as to how often you should change it. The answer could well be, 'every five years, whether it needs it or not.'

The benefits of stainless rigging are obvious in modern yachts. It is clean, it is very strong for its weight, and until it breaks, it is highly predictable from an engineering stand-point. None of these plus factors are relevant to the traditional gaffer, though the owners of modern traditional craft may feel they make sense.

Weight aloft is less of a problem for a gaffer, built on the understanding that she would suffer plenty of it all her days. She can therefore ship over-sized galvanised wire, and be absolutely certain it is strong enough. She may well have brown sails, so a little 'grunge' rubbing onto them from the rigging is not so serious.

Now the winnings begin to pile up. Galvanised wire is cheap. It requires no expensive terminal fittings which may carry away. It can be seized and spliced. It looks 'right', and, most important of all, its condition can be ascertained by a quick visual check. If it begins to show signs of surface rusting, scrape a small area ($^1/_4$in is plenty) and see if the wire immediately below the surface is bright. It probably will be, but if it isn't, further investigation will be required. Rust is something everyone understands. Molecular disturbance and hairline fractures are for the experts.

MAINTAINING GALVANISED WIRE

It doesn't matter who you talk to, they'll all give you a different 'only way' to treat galvanised wire. In the extravagant past, we were encouraged to leave our standing rigging coiled loosely inside a drum of boiled linseed oil, which would be heated gently for a number of days. For anything I know, there is no better treatment, if you can manage it.

Somewhat more realistic was the recommendation to dissolve grease in petrol, then work the mixture into the lay of the wire with a brush. The theory here was that the petrol sought the heart of the rope and then evaporated, leaving the grease behind. I have no quarrel with this per se, but I don't like petrol. Neither am I over-keen on leaving grease on my rigging.

I used to mix one part boiled linseed oil (It must be boiled. If it's raw, it never goes off), with one part of Stockholm Tar. This took about a week to skin, but worked well. It had the advantage of blackening the wire, which looks good. The time factor was the problem. Once, it didn't go off at all. The complaints lasted a year.

A liberal application of straight boiled linseed oil twice a year seems a simple and satisfactory solution. Over the seasons, it builds up in the lay until the wire presents an impervious surface to the water.

Forestays are extremely important items to maintain. Their surface galvanising doesn't last long, because it is knocked off by the staysail hanks. Fortunately, it is simplicity itself to run an oily rag up and down every few weeks during the season. It only takes ten minutes to send a hand up in the bosun's chair on the staysail halyard. He can hank the chair onto the forestay, then treat the wire as he comes down. If you can't find a volunteer, you'll have to knot an oily rag around the stay, attach it to the halyard, and bend on a downhaul. Run it up and down a few times. Spread a tarpaulin on the foredeck first, though, or the job will grow in ways you didn't want.

SERVING SPLICES

Unlike that of a modern yacht, a gaffer's rigging is full of splices. In the bad old days of natural fibre, these could all be attractively and neatly tapered, both for appearance and security. Alas, nothing in this life ever comes free of charge. Modern ropes are now almost universally selected for the reasons discussed in Chapter XVI, but they are, for the most part, utter misery to splice. The finished work is unlikely to be half so attractive as its counterpart of fifty years ago. Of course, in those days, there was no 'burning off the ends' for added sureness that the splice would not pull, so if it really counted, a splice was usually served, to make sure it stayed put.

It is still worth serving splices, then black varnishing the service, for cosmetic reasons, if nothing else. Splices in pre-stretched polyester are unattractive compared with their hempen equivalents, so anything that can make them less offensive will improve the appearance of the rig.

Certain rope companies now produce 'hemp look-alikes'. These are worth serious consideration, but be careful. Some are based on the dreaded polypropylene fibre, which the sun eats for its breakfast, dinner and tea.

MOUSING HOOKS

Traditional gaff rig gear made great use of forged iron hooks. Peak halyard blocks were hooked to the spans. They were often hooked to the mast as well. Reef pendants were hooked onto the reefing tackle, purchases were hooked to deck-eyes, and so on.

It is a sensible rule to mouse all hooks with a twist of wire, so that should the weight come off them unexpectedly, they will remain in place. Laziness about this small task has caused me a number of alarming midnight incidents. Once, when beating into a harbour in a gale of wind, my mainsheet came unhooked from the horse. It nearly cost me my ship.

Certain blocks, however, which one usually sees moused, never seem to give any trouble. I do not mouse my peak halyard blocks to the spans, or my throat halyard block to the gaff jaws, yet neither has come unhooked in 25 years. Idlers on quay walls advise me gratuitously that I should attend to the job, but I'm beginning to think that I may have been right all along. The reason I ignore these blocks is that the tiny jags of wire which may be left sticking out, despite my best endeavours, could catch the light cloth of the topsail. On the other hand, of course, when hoisting the topsail to windward, its foot has been known to snag in the jaws of unmoused hooks when we pulled on the sheet. If they'd been moused it would not have happened, so perhaps I should wire them up after all. But those blocks are on and off frequently for hoisting dinghies aboard, for heaving up lanyards, and for accommodating sail covers, so what do you think? I'm hanged if I know.

LAZY JACKS

When I think of the years I have suffered big gaff mainsails without lazy jacks, for the excellent reasons described below, I am tickled to death to see 32ft Bermudan sloops bothering with them. If you can't cope with 180sq ft of polyester without assistance, it's time you took up watching TV.

Despite my personal prejudices, lazy jacks can be a real help in a gaffer, so long as you can live with the trade-offs. They are easily rigged by splicing them into the twin topping lifts. Some boats carry them in two parts, knotted under the boom. If they are long enough they can then be tied up around the sail, doing away with any need for sail ties. On large American sloops they are often sensibly employed to help control the staysails.

The idea of lazy jacks is to form a net into which the sail will initially drop when it is lowered. They do this usefully enough, but they get in the way of the rolling process for making a really neat stow, the sail can hang up on them as it descends, and they add significantly to the counter-productive windage of the rig. If you think these a fair trade, you'd better order a set. Short-handed skippers may well be pleased they did. Even if you are fully crewed, a single pair rigged right aft to contain the gaff end can be worth a great deal.

RATLINES

Many people feel that a gaff-rigged vessel is incomplete without at least one set of ratlines (pronounced ratlins). This is true if she sets her topsails from aloft, and many larger vessels do just this. If it is not necessary to send a hand up the mast at sea on a regular basis, fitting ratlines is purely a matter of choice.

Significantly, few working craft or traditional yachts used ratlines, unless the boat fell into the category we have just defined. They were only rigged in small boats whose crew often required a view from aloft. The reason, of course, is the '3 Ws': windage, weight and work. It takes a lot of effort to 'rattle down' your shrouds. When the job is complete, you have succeeded in adding extra pounds to the weight of your rig, and increased the dreaded windage of a vessel which has so little performance to give away.

Nonetheless, when it comes to servicing the rig, ratlines are extremely useful. If this be the reason for installing them, they only need be rigged on one side. Make it starboard. If you need to go aloft at sea, you'll be heaving to for certain. You may as well be hove-to on the starboard tack, so that you have right of way over most other boats.

Ratlines really come into their own if you are proposing to cruise in icy waters, or among the coral reefs. In both of these, 'eyeball navigation' is essential, and the extra height makes a dramatic difference to your capacity to spot leads a mile away, or to peer down into the tropic sea to discern the awful brown of the shoals. For these purposes, I have rigged ratlines on two of my boats, starboard side only. On odd occasions, they have turned out to be on the wrong side, but in the main, the saving in the 3 Ws has set off the inconvenience.

Rigging Ratlines

A ratline is rigged by measuring the width between two shrouds, and splicing a soft eye into each end of a length of suitable rope so that it exactly fills the gap. The eyes are seized to the shrouds with racking seizings. Marline is excellent for this job, but black nylon fisherman's twine is even better.

If you have three shrouds per side, and you want to encompass them all, individual ratlines are clove-hitched around the central wire. The fore-and-aft ends are treated as before. Rope ratlines should begin life running parallel to the sheerpoles*. If they subsequently sag in the middle from heavy use, let them, but don't build the sag in. There'll be more than enough of that by the end of the season.

Sometimes ratlines are made up of wooden battens seized to the shrouds. The benefits are considerable from the climber's point of view. From every other aspect they are undesirable: more weight, more windage, etc. Still, they continue to be popular, particularly in the US. The best compromise is probably to place a wooden ratline every fourth or fifth step. This serves to stabilise the shrouds. It also provides a secure stopping place if you are only going half-way up for a look round.

If your shrouds are thin, particularly if they are of stainless steel wire, your seizings may tend to slip down. It used to be easy to solve this problem by binding the wire with a few turns of old-fashioned insulating tape in way of the seizing. PVC tape is useless for this, and I have yet to discover a substitute for the traditional 'friction tape'. Fortunately, one is never too old to learn, so I await enlightenment.

TANNING A FLAX SAIL

In the days when flax was king, working sailors went to great lengths to cutch, or tan-bark their sails. The processes undoubtedly increased the life of the canvas, and, if you have a flax sail today, you should think seriously about treating it.

The traditional systems were individualistic, and were very much on the 'eye of toad, leg of newt' principle. Such imaginative ingredients as Brazil wood, cochineal, alum and potassium bichromate were required by the text-books of the day. If this hi-tech approach failed to please, cauldrons of oak cuttings were to be boiled and reduced, before adding the sails, which were left to simmer for many hours. In the event of your timetable being too full to accommodate such a fussy affair, various more raunchy methods were recommended by locals operating their craft on the fringes of the known world, such as Arabia and North Yorkshire. There, essence of cowpat was a favoured preservative.

By far superior to any of these systems is a liberal application of 'Canvo', a commercially produced preservative. This excellent product comes in a variety of tasteful shades and is, or was the last time I needed any, sold in jumbo-sized cans. You paint it onto the sail, allow a reasonable time for drying off, then bend 'em on and go for it. There is a minimum of unpleasantness, and the canvas is left soft, supple, and a joy to behold. The treatment lasts for several years.

STRETCHING IN NATURAL FIBRE SAILS

1 — Choose your day carefully. No rain or fog, wind force 2/3.

2 — Bend on the sail. Outhaul the peak and clew until the wrinkles just disappear from the head and the foot. Do not overdo this on any account. Occasionally, the bolt-rope will be tight, in which case you'll have to pull harder to get rid of the wrinkles. Whatever you do, take it easy.

3 — Top well up.

4 — Hoist until the luff is gently tight, then peak up so that the usual tack-to-peak crease appears, but only just.

5 — Slack off the topping lift carefully, watching the sail. If creases appear between clew and throat, top up and heave another foot or so on the peak halyard. Try again until the sail looks smooth.

6 — Sail away and reach backwards and forwards. Don't come close-hauled because this dramatically increases the force on the sail.

7 — As you sail, wrinkles will appear at foot, luff and head. The first two can be hauled out while the canvas is working. The wrinkles in the head will have to wait until you can lower the sail, take them out, and start again. Do not heave away willy-nilly.

8 — The job should be complete by the end of a long summer's day. The minimum time in such a breeze is 5 or 6 hours — more if the weather is cold.

9 — On no account reef a sail that has not been stretched in. It will never be the same again.

The principles of tremendous caution apply to topsails and headsails, but if a jib has a wire luff, that part of the sail will already have been stretched by the sailmaker.

Sails of man-made fibre theoretically need no stretching in. Even so, you should try to go easy on them in their first few hours of use. Watch them, ensure that there are no stress points, and try not to reef them until they've had a day or so to settle in.

ADMIRALTY MANUAL

You will have noticed that this book contains little of what one might call 'marlinspike seamanship'. Although knots, splices, sewing, working cringles and the rest form a serious part of the life of the gaff rig sailor, they have all been covered so comprehensively elsewhere that to re-iterate the information seems superfluous. Nothing has changed for 100 years on the traditional materials front. Where modern materials have taken over, specialised techniques are rarely required, or, if they are, they are not exclusive to traditional rigs.

I therefore recommend that every gaffer, new or old, should carry aboard a copy of the Admiralty Manual of Seamanship; the more out-of-date it is, the better. The pre-World War II copies are solid gold. Many's the time I've sat on the saloon floor in mid-ocean, my battered old blue copy held open by the bosun's bag and an oak block, working a hand-laid cringle into the leech of a sail 'according to Lord Nelson'. The book is clear, it is written by greater experts than I, on that side of the business at least, and I cannot better it.

If you don't have one, begin scouring the second-hand bookshops now.

APPENDIX II

NOTES

4 POINTS Before World War II, most compasses were marked up in 'points' rather than degrees. Thus 000° became North, 090° East, etc. The cardinal points were each subdivided eight times which make a single compass point the equivalent of our 11¼ °. Four points represented 45°, 5 was about 55°. In many ways it is easier to think that way. This might sound crazy to our numerically organised minds, but to a seaman of Drake's or Cooke's day it was far more comprehensible. Sailing boats don't steer to the nearest degree in any case, so the points system made a great deal of sense.

If you are pinched up as close as 4 points from the wind, and decide to bear away to get her going, a helm order of 'knock her off half a point,' is far more relevant than a bleated, 'Try sailing 4° or 5° further off the wind.'
Give it a go. You'll be pleased with the results.

ALL STANDING A term of description relating to any action taken without proper preparation. Thus, to gybe all standing, is to allow the boom to crash across without any attempt to control it on the mainsheet. An all standing gybe in the grandest sense would involve backstays left made up. In such a case the results could prove catastrophic.

ARCHER, COLIN 1832–1921. Born in Norway of Scottish parents, he was perhaps the greatest designer of working vessels of all time. Boats are still built to his concepts. His life-saving craft have never been beaten for seaworthiness, while his pilot boats were a glory of speed, beauty and strength. Sadly, his name is often taken in vain, and many, though not all, so-called 'Colin Archer types' are fat, ugly sluggards.

BAGGYWRINKLE Chafing gear suitable for rigging along a rope or wire. It forms a 'furry' pad and is generally seen on shrouds, backstays and topping lifts. It is made by stretching out a double length of marline, and cow-hitching a series of 6–8in lengths of old rope yarn to it. Wrapped tightly around the rope in question it forms a cylindrical pad which is very effective.

BECKET The fitting on a block to which a rope may be attached.

BIGHT The middle part of a rope, between the belay and the load. Sometimes the term is used to define a loop of rope, or even a loop of the coastline as in 'German Bight'.

BITTS   These are massive baulks of timber, stepped deep down in the vessel (ideally on the keel), with their upper ends protruding through the foredeck. They are used for the bowsprit heel and sometimes form the basis of a traditional windlass, as well as being excellent for towing or tying up.

BRAIL   These are ropes which serve to gather up a standing gaff sail or a spritsail, spilling wind from it and stowing it against the mast and the gaff. They run inboard from the leech of the sail to turning blocks on the spars. They are handled from the deck.

BULLDOG GRIPS   These are really a highly-developed form of U-bolt for holding two wires firmly together. They can be used to make a permanent job, and boats have circumnavigated (notably Bernard Moitessier in *Joshua*) with nothing but bulldogs to hold the rigging together.

BULLSEYE   A fair-lead made of a sphere of hardwood, drilled and chamfered for the rope to pass through. The outside of the sphere is scored all round to take a strop which may be of rope or iron. Bullseyes are usually of lignum vitae.

CAMBER   The flow, or curvature of a sail when seen in a cross section cut at right-angles to the mast. The maximum camber should be about 40% of the way from luff to leech on most sails.

CHAIN PLATES   Standing rigging attachment points in hull or deck. Their name relates to their origins, when they stood proud of the hull (as channels), supported from below by chains.

CHEEK BLOCK   A single sheave built onto the side of a spar.

CLUB   A 'club' is a short spar laced to the aft end of the foot of a sail which is otherwise loose-footed. It serves two main functions. One is to extend the sail beyond its natural sheeting position, thus gaining area. The other, which is really a spin-off, is that the operator has a choice of attaching the sheet anywhere along the club, which assists in the search for a good sheet-lead.

Clubs are used on staysails for sloops, and sometimes on a loose-footed schooner foresail, but they are found more commonly on the foot of a topsail, where they are sometimes known as 'jackyards'.

CRANE   A fitting for holding the upper throat halyard block well out abaft the mast.

CRANSE IRON   A hoop of iron driven onto a shoulder at the outboard end of the bowsprit. For a fully rigged spar the cranse would have four lugs (small rings) welded to it for the attachment of standing rigging.

FALL   That part of a purchase which is pulled by the operator. A double-ended halyard has two falls. One is the hauling end, by which the sail is taken aloft. The other is the standing end, on which is rigged a further purchase, supplying the tension for the whole assembly.

FIDDED TOPMAST   An extension upwards of a mast, so called because it is stopped from descending by a fid, or iron spike upon which it sits, or which is passed through its lower sections.

FOREFOOT   The part of a vessel's underwater profile between the stem and the straight part of the keel. If the keel never does straighten out, as is the case with certain yachts, it can be considered as the part of the underwater form forward of the mast.

FULL-RIGGED SHIP   Any 3-masted vessel which is square-rigged on all three masts is technically a 'ship'. Any other permutations of sails places a vessel into a different category, such as barque, barquentine, three-masted topsail schooner, etc.

GAMMON IRON   The hoop at the stem through which the bowsprit is passed. The term goes back to the days when bowsprits were lashed down to the stem by a system of well-organised ropework called gammoning.

GASKET   A sail tie which is kept permanently rigged. These are favoured in places where the crew may be hanging on by one hand for themselves, with only one left for the ship, such as square yards and bowsprits.

GOOSE-NECK   The metal fitting which supplies universal movement between boom and mast. Some booms do not have a goose-neck, preferring instead a set of jaws similar to those of the gaff. These sit on a wooden shelf around the mast when at rest.

HANDY BILLY   A travelling tackle which can be set up wherever extra purchase is needed. The stationary block often has a useful shackle or hook, while the moving block carries a lanyard which is rolling hitched to the rope to be pulled.

HELM 'DOWN' AND 'UP'   The term applies to the way a tiller, if there is one, would be pushed for any particular manoeuvre. For example, the helm is put down (to leeward) when the boat tacks. It is put up (to windward) for a gybe. The terminology passes through unchanged to wheel steering. Regardless of which way the wheel is turned, the helm is still put 'down' if the boat is to turn to windward, and vice-versa.

HORSE   A sort of bridge set above the deck or a boom, through-bolted at both ends, along which an attachment may slide. The horse for a mainsail clew would be of iron, and the main part of its length (about 18in on a 21ft boom) runs parallel to the upper surface of the boom. Horses are also used for sheets, notably mainsheets and staysail sheets. Sheet horses run athwartships and are also usually of iron, though exceptionally they may be of heavy timber, as in the Thames sailing barge.

HOUNDS   That part of the mast to which the main shrouds are attached. In a gaffer it is well up the shaft, because it must be above the gaff jaws.

JACKYARD   See 'Club'

JIB-BOOM   An extension to the bowsprit of a basically similar form to a topmast. It is held in place by spectacle irons (see note), and carries a full set of shrouds and stays. It does not normally bear a vessel's main forestay.

JIB-HEADED   As the name suggests, a jib-headed sail is pointed at the top. It is entirely innocent of yards or headsticks.

LEG-OF-MUTTON   A picturesque old term for the 3-cornered boomed sail. It is often used with reference to a bermudan mizzen on a gaff ketch.

LIFTING   The luff of a sail is said to lift when it first begins to be backwinded.

OVERHAUL   The friction inherent in any tackle makes pulling it out by heaving on one of its blocks hard work. If the rope is worked through beforehand so that the tackle lies slack, the job becomes very much easier. This process is known as overhauling. Sometimes, all that is necessary to overhaul is to let off the fall of a purchase before a sail is dropped, but if you want slack on the mainsheet before topping up the boom, you'll have to pull it through as described.

PARBUCKLE   A simple means of achieving a purchase. It works on the same principle as a whip, but instead of using a block, the rope is passed around the load itself. Parbuckling is also a useful way of raising a heavy spar or barrel up a vessel's side from the water.

PARREL BALLS   Small, hardwood spheres drilled to accept a rope.

PEAK   The top aft corner of the gaff sail. The peak halyards raise the aft part of the gaff. They also control the angle the spar is making with the mast.

PENDANT   Sometimes PENNANT. A rope which serves to haul down the clew reef cringle, or ear-ring.

PURCHASE   The tackle rigged to the standing end of a two-ended halyard.

RACKING SEIZING   A seizing designed so that only one of the two wires seized together takes the load.

RINGTAIL   An extension which is rigged at the leech of a gaff mainsail. It requires light spars to be arranged on gaff and boom to carry its head and foot. These sails are almost never seen nowadays.

SEIZING   A seizing is a sophisticated form of lashing which holds two ropes or wires together, side by side.

SHEAVE   The wheel part of a pulley block. Sometimes a sheave is let into a spar, as in the case of the main clew outhaul or the bowsprit traveller outhaul.

SHEERPOLE   The sheerpoles run fore-and-aft, joining together the shrouds immediately above the upper dead-eyes or the rigging screws. They can be lashed or bolted on. Their official function is to stop the shrouds from sheering, or twisting, but they also serve as useful places to carry belaying pins from which to hang halyards at sea. They form a conveniently sturdy bottom step for the ratlines.

SPAN   A strop of served wire or rope, attached by looping round the gaff in two places. A single halyard block is hooked to a fitting (often a bullseye) which can run on the span.
   Two spans is the normal thing normal in vessels over 30ft, while on extremely large craft three is not uncommon. The span has two advantages: no bolt need be driven through the spar, and it serves to spread out the load of the peak halyards.

SPECTACLE IRONS   These are the two iron double hoops (although the lower one may be square) which form the doublings supporting the topmast or jib-boom. They are given this name because the round upper fitting looks exactly like a giant pince-nez if you lay it down on deck.

STOPPER   In this instance, the stopper is a length of rope rolling hitched to the bight of the halyard, with possibly a couple more half hitches around to back up the main hitch. To be really sure, the stopper can be wormed round with the lay before leaving the halyard after a final half-hitch. The end of the stopper is now hauled tight and belayed. It will hold the bight of the halyard until it has been belayed; then the stopper is let off and removed.
   The principle of the stopper has numerous applications.

SURGE   To allow a loaded rope to render around a cleat or bollard under control.

TACKLE   Pronounced 'taykle', this is an arrangement of blocks (pulleys) and ropes, rove up to give a mechanical advantage.

THROAT The upper forward corner of a gaff sail is always known as the throat. Thus, the throat halyard is the forward of the two gaff halyards.

TOPPING LIFT A rope which supports the weight of the boom when it is not being carried by the sail.

TOPSAIL YARD The spar attached to the luff of the yard topsail. This is not to be confused with the jackyard, though it frequently is.

TRAVELLER In this context a traveller is a forged, leathered ring which runs up and down around the bowsprit.

TRIATIC STAY Fore-and-aft support between a schooner's lower mastheads. This vital wire supplies forestaying for the mainmast while on the wind and some backstaying for the foremast with the breeze well aft. The names of schooner topmast stays vary in different countries, but they generally live up to one's expectations. In North America the springstay and the freshwater are often favoured.

TRUCK The wooden cap which protects the end grain of a timber mast.

VANG In traditional craft a vang is a rope which controls the movement of the outboard end of a gaff or sprit. Sprit rigs have two of these, one each side, and sailors pronounce them as wangs. Gaff vangs are pronounced as spelt, and generally only one is rigged per spar.

WHIP A single block hanging from a rope. By reeving a line through it and dead-ending one end, the resulting power which is applied to the load is 2:1. Whips are effective because with only one sheave involved, friction is cut to a minimum.

Index